MW01259366

THE PARTHENON
COOKBOOK

THE PARTHENON

COOKBOOK

GREAT MEDITERRANEAN RECIPES FROM THE HEART OF CHICAGO'S GREEKTOWN

CAMILLE STAGG

S
SURREY
BOOKS

CHICAGO

Copyright 2008 The Parthenon Restaurant

All rights reserved. No part of this book may be reproduced or transmitted in any form or by any means, electronic or mechanical, including photocopying, recording, or by any information storage and retrieval system, without express written permission from the publisher.

Book design and layout: Brandtner Design

Food photography copyright 2008 by Richard Foreman. All rights reserved. Used with permission.
Page 10 photograph by Mark Mamalakis. Image courtesy of the Hellenic Museum and Cultural Center, Chicago, Ilinois.

Printed in China.

First edition.

Library of Congress Cataloging-in-Publication Data

The Parthenon cookbook : great Greek recipes from the heart of Chicago's Greektown / Camille Stagg.

    p. cm.

Summary: "A tribute to Chicago's Parthenon Restaurant, including a collection of Greek recipes, wine pairings, and menu suggestions"--Provided by publisher.

ISBN-13: 978-1-57284-096-6 (hardcover)

ISBN-10: 1-57284-096-X (hardcover)

1. Cookery, Greek. 2. Parthenon (Restaurant) I. Title.

TX723.5.G8S72 2008

641.59495--dc22

                  2 0 0 8 0 1 0 8 6 7

10 9 8 7 6 5 4 3 2 1

Surrey Books is an imprint of Agate Publishing. Surrey and Agate books are available in bulk at discount prices. For more information, visit gatepublishing.com

Dedication

For the people in my life who have influenced everything:

My parents, Panagiotis, who helped me rebuild the restaurant,
and Yannoula, who gave me life and sustained me through hard times.

My children, Yanna and Peter, whom I love, and who have stood beside
me day in and day out at the restaurant and for any life decisions I make.

My wife Lorraine, whom I love;
she has always helped me, no matter how crazy my requests have been.

My brothers Bill, who was there from the beginning with me,
and George, who helped me become the man I am.
My sister Chrisoula, who has loved and supported me throughout my life.

My business partners, past and present.
My restaurant staff, past and present,
who have helped shape the Parthenon into the great restaurant it is today:

My devoted friends… one of whom is this book's author:
And, most importantly…..

My loyal and loving customers and their families,
who have supported The Parthenon all these years!

TABLE OF CONTENTS

PREFACE:
ABOUT THE PARTHENON RESTAURANT
AND THIS BOOK

A SYMBOL OF THE BIRTHPLACE OF WESTERN civilization, the Parthenon is one of Greece's proudest achievements. It is the focal point of the most famous collection of buildings in history, standing majestically atop Athens's Acropolis.

Naming our restaurant after this architectural wonder carries a deep responsibility for excellence; we will never take this responsibility lightly. We hope that in some small way, our efforts will help you to know the pure enjoyment of the Greek dining experience.

— **Chris Liakouras**

INTRODUCTION

GREECE IS A CHARMED (AND CHARMING), TIMELESS COUNTRY THAT INVITES exploration of its rich culture and wealth of history. With their amazing scenery and quaint small towns (some of which were once powerful city-states), Greece's mainland and 1.500 islands are closely connected to the sea and sun. Contemporary Greece links the spirits of previous civilizations to present-day life.

Greece's capital, Athens, is crowned by the Parthenon temple, which is dedicated to the goddess of wisdom, Athena (of course, the city itself is named for her). We think of Greece as the cornerstone of Western civilization and the birthplace of democracy. However, it is actually the crossroads of the West and the East, and since ancient times, Greece was influenced more by the East.

Among my most memorable travel experiences are the weeks I've spent in Greece: Viewing the remarkable architecture of the stately Parthenon in Athens; dining outdoors at tavernas in the Plaka, Athens's old quarter, at the foot of the Acropolis; listening to *bouzouki* music; taking the Classical tour and walking in the footsteps of ancient Greeks amid the historic ruins, including the site of the Olympics; cruising the Aegean Sea; viewing the powerful fortifications surrounding the old city of Rhodes; riding a mule up the hills of the beautiful island of Santorini; and sipping coffee at outdoor cafes on picturesque Mykonos, with its famous windmills. Simple pleasures, such as eating fresh figs with feta on a beach, are among my most treasured memories.

Greeks tend to be very proud of their ancient roots (and rightly so). The culture is rich and steeped in tradition, including everything from traditional dances to special holiday foods. Perhaps the most cherished holiday foods are those for Greek Easter, including red-dyed Easter eggs, whole lambs on roasting spits (the first meat eaten since the start of Lent, forty days earlier), and delicious Easter breads.

Just as the original Parthenon in Athens evolved through the ages, so has The Parthenon restaurant in Chicago's Greektown. It is a remarkable success story, opening with a staff of three and growing to today's full staff of more than 50 employees.

IT'S NO SURPRISE THAT THE PARTHENON AND ITS OWNERS, THE LIAKOURAS family, have garnered numerous awards and great reviews over the past forty years. In a time when many restaurants have a short life span, it is encouraging to see such longevity. The Parthenon is the oldest restaurant in Chicago's Greektown, and celebrates its fortieth anniversary on July 5, 2008.

Chris Liakouras founded the restaurant with his brother, Bill, who now lives in Athens. The brothers popularized gyros in the U.S. and invented flaming saganaki. (Parthenon waiters shout "Oopa!" as they flambé saganaki with brandy, a house specialty.) Chris Liakouras has continued to expand the business, working with his daughter, Yanna (the restaurant's managing partner); his son, Peter (restaurant manager); Sotiris Stasinos (partner and chef); and the rest of the dedicated staff of The Parthenon as the restaurant enters its fifth decade.

The menu has a great assortment of *mezedes* (a substantial sampling of small dishes), many of which are offered in different portion sizes or as a combination. This basic concept is ideally suited to the Greek cultural sense of *filoxenia* (hospitality) and the centuries-old tradition of getting together with friends to sample many dishes, drink wine, and talk. Other house specialties include homemade gyros; barbecued lamb (you can watch them turn on spits in the restaurant's window); Greek-style whole red snapper or sea bass; and Athenian broiled chicken.

Enjoy Chapter 1's timeline, which highlights some of the most special occasions and milestones in the restaurant's four decades of history. Chris Liakouras, who has an amazing encyclopedic memory, revealed much of the history of the evolution of Greektown as his own restaurant developed and grew—all with fascinating anecdotes along the way. Many of The Parthenon's staff are longtime employees; you'll find some of their memories in the pages of Chapter 2. Also, you'll learn about the Liakouras family's vision of the future for The Parthenon and for Greektown. The Parthenon's tradition of constantly expanding and improving will never change. The future is bright!

For those Parthenon devotees who have been requesting recipes over the years (and for newcomers who love the food too), the owners share 50 of their recipes in Chapter 3. The recipes were selected for their adaptability to a home kitchen. The chapter also includes information about Greek cuisine, and a helpful food glossary follows Chapter 4. The recipes have been tested by several home cooks (including, in many cases, myself). Yanna and the chef gave final approval on every one, so we are confident you will enjoy them with your family and friends.

Chapter 4 is a wonderful reference for Greek-style entertaining. It includes Greek menus with wine suggestions, wine pairing information, and entertaining tips. The quality and variety of Greek wines has expanded and improved dramatically over the years, so you will be able to find just the right wine for any meal!

There is only one Parthenon, the anchor of Chicago's Greektown, but the community's other fine Greek restaurants deserve a salute for their special contribution to the city. Greektown is like no other place. May this cookbook bring you much reading, cooking, and dining pleasure!

Efharisto! (Thank you!) — ***Camille Stagg***

THE HELLENIC MUSEUM AND CULTURAL CENTER

The Hellenic Museum and Cultural Center, the cultural anchor of Greektown, supplied many of the photos in the historical chapters of this book. We invited Sophia Kintis, the Museum's Executive Director, to offer some notes on the role of food and culture in the life of Chicago's Greek community:

THE FOODS WE EAT HAVE A HISTORY, AND OUR CHOICES ARE SHAPED BY WHO we are, where we reside, and how we live our lives. Food is deeply embedded in the rituals of daily life, intimately linked with culture, and entwined with identity. It nourishes culture. Familiar foods from childhood can evoke memories of warmth and comfort. Parents express affection by preparing home-cooked meals, and sharing those meals with strangers extends the family's embrace. Food marks important moments in our personal lives and defines us as a community. We include food in celebrations of reverence, of joy, and of sorrow.

Food has also played an important role in the story of Greek immigration to Chicago and the evolution of Greek-American culture. In the late 19th century, crusty loaves of bread, tangy olives, and pungent garlic reminded lonely male immigrants of their sun-baked villages and loved ones left behind. At the same time, cheeseburgers, milkshakes, and apple pie provided ambitious entrepreneurs with an avenue to economic independence and the ability to reunite their families and put down roots in the city.

Through the years, American foods dominated the menus of many Greek-owned restaurants, but at home, the tastes and aromas of Greek foods reinforced traditional values and provided a connection to distant shores. As they negotiated between these two culinary worlds, immigrants and their children developed new Greek-American traditions and nourished an emerging Greek-American identity.

Greektown's historic Parthenon Restaurant remains an anchor for the Greek community. It is a symbol of the dedication of immigrants and their enduring spirit.

—Sophia Kintis
Executive Director, Hellenic Museum and Cultural Center

For the past two decades, the Hellenic Museum and Cultural Center (HMCC) has offered a vibrant and comprehensive picture of Greece's art and history and of Greek communities in the U.S. The Museum has a longstanding history of producing fascinating original exhibitions, ranging from ancient Greek civilizations to contemporary artwork. The exhibitions presented over the years have interpreted Hellenic history and culture in an effort to preserve knowledge and stimulate appreciation of Greek culture. HMCC continually strives to carefully integrate historic Hellenic content in a much broader context, presenting a universal and relevant message about Greece, its people, and its history to the public.

FOREWORD
Filotimo on Halsted Street

SATURDAY NIGHT ON HALSTED STREET. THE NEON LIGHTS FROM THE FACADES of restaurants glitter across the arriving cars. As a young valet takes my car, I admire the adroit way he maneuvers it through the stream of traffic, swiftly parking it so he can race back for another car.

In the window of The Parthenon, a succulent, browning lamb turns slowly on a spit, stimulating my appetite. The restaurant is a clamorous enclave that blends voices, the lilting melodies of Greek music, and the aromas of savory food. A host seats me, and a busboy brings me a glass of water. A young waiter, handsome as Apollo (if that deity had raven black hair), brings me a menu and flashes a smile.

"Our special tonight is lamb with artichokes," he says. "Would you like something to drink?"

I order a glass of roditis, study the menu, and glance around at the patrons occupying the tables around me. There are many young people from the University of Illinois campus and other young people from elsewhere in the city, their natural energy made even more buoyant by the surroundings. There are older patrons, as well, and families with children. A waiter approaches an adjoining table with several trays of saganaki stacked on his arm. He lights the brandy on the cheese with a flourish, and as the flame flares, he cries, "Ooopppa!" The tone for the evening is set and I get down to the business of selecting and enjoying my dinner.

I cannot count the number of visits I have made to Halsted Street in the last five decades, the numerous meals I have eaten at various Greek restaurants, and the glasses of roditis or retsina I have drunk. I know the warmth of those visits lingers with me for days.

Considering the many restaurants on Halsted where I have eaten so well, it would be imprudent to declare that one is the best. That would be a disservice to many fine establishments. But certainly, I can say that one of my true favorites is The Parthenon.

Part of my attachment has to do with the length of time I have been eating there. Brothers Chris and Bill Liakouras opened the Parthenon in 1968, and my first visit to the restaurant was in that year or in the year after. In the following decades, The Parthenon has hosted many of our family dinners. We have celebrated birthdays and numerous holiday gatherings there. Our family reunions in 1995, 2000, and 2005, which brought together seventy-five to eighty relatives from across the U.S. to Chicago for three days, always began with an evening at The Parthenon. Some of the most convivial celebrations heralding the publication of my books have taken place at The Parthenon.

Among the hosts I remember most fondly are the courteous John Sarikas and the courtly Gregory Karabis. And always, a warm greeting from Chris, the reassuring clasp of his big hand, and the effusiveness and affection of his smile.

As Chris Liakouras and I have grown older together, our bond of friendship has remained warm and firm. As the restaurant has grown, its seating increased and banquet rooms added, Chris has been joined in the business by his daughter, Yanna, and son, Peter. Daughter and son continue the gracious Parthenon tradition of making each guest feel like a celebrity.

There is a word in Greek, *filotimo*, that is difficult to translate, but it conveys the special esteem one has for visitors. Once, as a stranger walking through a village in Greece, I was greeted and invited into almost every house, offered a sweet *loukoumi* and a glass of cool water. I felt as welcome as a relative.

My good friends at The Parthenon, as well as in the other restaurants that adorn Halsted Street, extend that *filotimo* beyond their homes and into their businesses, where both young and old savor Greek food and wine, and provide the special hospitality toward strangers that marks the Greek psyche.

In the course of world events and calamities wrought by humans and nature alike, it might be presumptuous to apportion too great a significance to the ritual of eating dinner on Halsted Street—however convivial and satisfying a restaurant's food and atmosphere might be. But within the pages of this book, let me record that although I have eaten in restaurants in Los Angeles, Denver, New York, Paris, London, Athens, Tokyo, Kuala Lumpur, and Hong Kong, if one asked me to name two or three favorites, The Parthenon would be on that list.

Long may its fine tradition flourish, and long may its saganaki flame to the ebullient cries of, "Ooooppa!" — ***Harry Mark Petrakis***

Acclaimed novelist Harry Mark Petrakis, the son of a Greek Orthodox priest, has been writing and lecturing for the last fifty years. He has won numerous awards including two nominations for the National Book Award in Fiction. His work has been adapted for film and TV, including the novel A Dream of Kings, *which was made into a major motion picture. His 21st book,* Legends of Glory and Other Stories, *was published in the spring of 2007.*

CHAPTER ONE
The Parthenon Timeline

TO COMMEMORATE THE PARTHENON'S thirtieth anniversary in 1998, Chris Liakouras asked me to write a pictorial booklet that would be a brief retrospective of his restaurant. I relished working on the project, because it meant interviewing Chris, taking notes, and taping his entertaining stories and funny anecdotes. I asked him for names of some friends and regular customers, and I followed up with them to get some quotes. After getting the glowing praises of these people—all of whom loved Chris—I had even greater admiration for Chris and his restaurant.

Later, my writing from the booklet was posted on The Parthenon's website, and ever since I've been pleased to see my words reused by various writers in different publications. Since this is my own original work, I am excerpting some of it here, entwined with new material. People love to return to The Parthenon because everyone has fun

Current partners Chris Liakouras (left), his daughter, Yanna, and chef Sotiris Stasinos.

PRICES AT THE PARTHENON IN 1968

An order of gyros: $2.95

A bottle of roditis: $1.95

An order of saganaki: $1.25

A family-style dinner: $3.95

The combination plate: $3.25

1968 FACTS

The average income in the United States is $7,844

Minimum wage is $1.60

A new house costs just under $15,000

A new car costs around $2,800

A gallon of gasoline costs $ .34

A loaf of bread costs $ .22

A first-class postage stamp costs $ .06

Richard Nixon is elected president of the United States, succeeding Lyndon Johnson

1968, JULY 5: The Parthenon opens its doors at 314 S. Halsted Street on Chris's birthday with three employees: Chef Angelo Gailas, who trained in Greece; co-owner Bill Liakouras, as bartender and manager; and co-owner Chris Liakouras, who is host, waiter, and busboy. The restaurant takes in $110 on its first day of business, and the business grows steadily thereafter.

1968, SEPTEMBER 14: The restaurant experiences its first line of waiting customers. Host Chris happily serves ouzo to those standing in line—the hospitable Greek way. During the first two years of business, the Liakouras brothers offer samples from the menu to each table to familiarize customers with their dishes.

1969: The first small expansion takes place, adding twenty more seats to the back room. The restaurant now seats 110 patrons.

1969, JUNE: A burglary proves helpful to the business. The Parthenon's safe is broken into and the thieves get away with about $14,000 in cash and checks. All the main television stations and several radio stations cover the burglary, which makes the restaurant even more popular. Many people dine at The Parthenon to support them through the crisis. In his television interviews, Bill is clearly very upset about the loss, but easygoing Chris was able to see the sunny side of things. Later, he said, "We couldn't have afforded that much media coverage. The burglary actually ended up being good for business!"

1971, SEPTEMBER: The Liakouras brothers buy the building next door to the south for their first big expansion, which adds another 190 seats. Within three years, The Parthenon more than triples its original size, with 300 seats.

OPPOSITE:
Peter Liakouras mans the gyros, which was popularized at The Parthenon.

1974: Chef Sotiris Stasinos arrives at The Parthenon to work in the kitchen with Chef Angelo Gailas. Several years later, when Gailas returns to Greece, Stasinos becomes the executive chef, and later a partner in the business.

1975, JULY 5: At the restaurant's seventh-anniversary dinner, the entire group is drinking Metaxa and having a great time. A photographer tries to capture Chris serving some flaming saganaki. The photographer directs Chris, saying, "Closer to the saganaki… to the left." Eventually, Chris gets too close, and his hair catches on fire (see photo, pp. 12-13). For a moment, he's unaware of what is happening, but all ends well, and he is unharmed. Chris advises that it's best to not get too close to flaming saganaki, and that for inner warmth, drink Metaxa—but do so cautiously.

1975: Later that same year, The Parthenon makes a record of Greek music and distributes the 6,000 copies as gifts. Chris and Bill are pictured on the cover. On the record, Chris delivers a special anniversary greeting and introduces the Greek music.

Bill returns to Greece with his family. John Sarikas is hired as the restaurant's manager. He will remain there as manager until 2001, when he retires.

1978: The Parthenon turns 10, already outlasting most restaurants.

1981: Several doors down, at Halsted and Van Buren, Chris opens Courtyards of Plaka. This lovely peach-hued restaurant with an outdoor courtyard features upscale Greek cuisine and live piano music. Six years later, Chris sells the restaurant to his manager, who changes its name to Costa's.

1988: The Parthenon celebrates its 20th birthday.

OPPOSITE:
Chris cuts a rug with actress Joey Heatherton, circa 1970.

BELOW:
Album graphics for a collection of Greek music produced as gifts for restaurant patrons.

1993, SPRING: The restaurant's interior and exterior get a facelift in anticipation of its 25th anniversary. A beautiful new sign is erected out front.

1993, JULY 5: The Parthenon celebrates 25 years in style with a big anniversary party featuring a lavish buffet, live music, and Greek dancing for its invited guests. Bill Liakouras and other family members travel from Greece for the celebration. Bill's son, Peter, is a managing partner at this time. T-shirts are made to serve as souvenirs for the occasion.

1995, FEBRUARY: Yanna joins her father, Chris, in the business as an assistant manager. She is very proud of her dad and is delighted to be working with him. Together, their hands-on management reinforces the strength of this family business. She says, "He's always treated me with respect—even

The Parthenon's beautiful banquet room, part of a number of expansions the restaurant has undergone over the past 40 years.

when I was a teenager, he made me feel like an adult." Chris is just as proud of his only daughter, and likes to say, "She's smarter than I am." Chris jokes that his daughter understands computers, but he doesn't even know how to turn them on. Later, Yanna becomes a managing partner in the business. When Bill Liakouras's son, Peter, sells his share and moves out of state, Chef Sotiris becomes a partner as well.

1996, MARCH: A chic new bar is added in the building next door to the north, connecting it to the original bar. The entryway to The Parthenon is now even more welcoming. A glass case displays Parthenon merchandise, including T-shirts, totes, and key chains.

1998, JULY 5: The Parthenon turns 30, standing proud and ready for the coming new millennium. Chris and Yanna continue their tradition of welcoming feedback from their customers and accommodating their wishes, as Chris vows that his restaurant will continue to evolve and expand, both in the menu and the seating capacity. The Liakouras family hosts a big party featuring a lavish buffet of specialties, a band, and lots of Greek dancing. *The Greek Star* newspaper publishes a wonderful illustrated feature about Chicago's oldest classic Greek restaurant.

1999: Chris's son, Peter, begins working in the restaurant as a manager and gracious host. Chris is delighted to have both his daughter and his son working with him.

2002, SEPTEMBER: A large banquet facility is added next door that can accommodate 150 to 200 people for a sit-down dinner and up to 250 people for a stand-up reception. The room includes two bars, a dance floor, and two large TVs anchored from the ceiling, making the room appropriate for everything from business meetings to parties. The Parthenon's regular menu, family-style dinner, banquet, and buffet menus are available in the banquet facility, along with open-bar packages. Groups can also book a three-piece band with belly dancers through the restaurant.

2003, JULY 5: The Parthenon celebrates 35 years with a grand party in its new banquet facility. The banquet room is aglow with colorful lights, balloons, flowers, food, and music as the Liakouras family and their guests celebrate this momentous occasion. Chris Liakouras, clad in a tuxedo, performs various Greek dances, and belly dancers circulate through the crowd. The *Greek Star* publishes another wonderful feature with photos after the event.

OPPOSITE:
*Dancers
at Chicago's
annual
Greek parade.*

2004, JUNE: A new catering menu is launched that allows customers to host their own Parthenon party at their homes or offices.

2004, AUGUST: The Parthenon salutes the return of the Olympic Games to its original home, Athens, with a special Olympic family-style dinner menu for two or more. The menu features saganaki, eggplant dip, barrel olives, Athenian salad, lamb chops, large shrimp, chicken breasts, shish kebobs, and spinach pie, as well as dessert and coffee. Runners carry the Olympic torch through Greektown. The Parthenon pays tribute to the 2004 Olympic Games by proudly displaying the Olympic flag next to its Greek flag in the lounge window and raising the Olympic flag outside after the Games begin. For a touch of whimsy, all the waiters wear Olympic medals.

2007, NOVEMBER: Another renovation takes place before the holiday season begins. The Parthenon doubles the size of its entrance and completely remodels the original bar, installing a new floor, ceiling, counters, and a back bar with lighting, chairs, and televisions. The new entryway is magnificent, with the remodeled bar to the left and the expanded bar a step up to the right. To everyone's delight, the rotisserie roast returns to the windows, where passersby can watch lambs, chickens, and pigs roast, and the gyros spin.

2008, JULY 5: The Parthenon celebrates its 40th anniversary with a grand party and the debut of its first cookbook, which features 50 favorite recipes from the menu. *The Parthenon Cookbook: Great Mediterranean Recipes from The Heart of Chicago's Greektown* also serves as a tribute to Chris; his partners, daughter Yanna Liakouras and chef Sotiris Stasinos; his son, manager-host Peter; and the rest of the dedicated staff.

CHAPTER TWO

The Parthenon and Greektown Since the 1960s: A Retrospective

ALTHOUGH MANY GREEKS LOVE THEIR homeland and find it very hard to leave family and friends behind, those who immigrated to America hope to make a fortune and a better life. Chris Liakouras and his brother, Bill, shared this dream, and were motivated to chart new territory on Chicago's Halsted Street. Their dream became reality when they opened The Parthenon.

FROM GREECE TO DETROIT

The Liakouras family is originally from Megalopoli, which sits in a large valley in the mountainous Peloponissos region of Greece. Today, the region's biggest claim to fame is that it produces electricity for all of southern Greece. Despite the colossal nature of its name, Megalopoli is bigger than a town, but smaller than most cities.

"There is not much wine made in my hometown, since grapes are grown on slopes, not in the moun-

Opaa! The famous photo of Chris catching fire in 1975, which spawned the slogan "We created flaming Saganaki… it took practice!" (Fortunately, Chris was not injured.)

tains," Chris emphasizes. "The Greek sausage with orange peel on our menu, *loukaniko*, is from Megalopoli."

In 1955, nineteen-year-old Chris arrived in the United States from Greece with his father and brother, Bill. They settled in Detroit, which has its own Greektown. The following year, Chris enlisted in the United States Army and was sent to Korea. He returned to the States in 1958.

Moving to Chicago from Detroit: The Roots of Greektown

"Shortly after I returned from Korea," Chris said, "My friend Petros Tzafaroglou and I left Detroit for Chicago with very little money, but we both quickly found jobs. In 1959, my brother Bill moved to Chicago to join me.

"We worked as waiters at a couple of places, including Dianna's Grocery and Restaurant, which was opened by the Kogiones brothers in 1961. At that time, it was the only Greek restaurant on Halsted Street, with tables in the back for about 80 people. They had a very limited menu—just dolmades and moussaka, and once a week, braised lamb; there was no saganaki or gyros. I worked there as a waiter for two to three years.

"Bill and I worked as waiters, saved our money, and dreamt of opening a restaurant in Halsted Street's Greektown, which already had several other Greek businesses. The opportunity arrived in 1968 when an existing Greek restaurant at 314 S. Halsted Street went on the market.

The Birth of The Parthenon

Chris continues, "I spoke with the owner of the existing restaurant, who was ready to sell. The venture didn't go well, but it wasn't the chef's fault. We finally negotiated the deal for $38,000 over a couple bottles of retsina. The restaurant closed on July 1, and on July 5, we opened The Parthenon. The former restaurant's chef, Angelo Gailas, had trained in Greece. He was a fine chef, and we kept him. I suggested to him what we wanted to

serve. Together, we worked on the recipes to develop a small menu. Gyros cooked on electric spits in those days. We put a whole lamb on a rotisserie in the window. We wanted fresh food daily—no leftovers. I told the chef not to worry about the budget for food, because freshness was too important.

"The business started growing quickly. On the first day, we took in $110, and on the second day, $200. When we bought the place, our father, Peter, did not know about it. After he learned about The Parthenon from others, he stopped by one day after work in the midafternoon to see the place for the first time. The restaurant was empty, so he suggested that we put a pool table in the middle of the place and shoot a game. I am a good pool player; I played

Founders Chris (left) and Bill Liakouras toasting Hollywood star Jane Russell, circa 1970.

all the time. This was his way of letting me know that he didn't appreciate finding out from others that his sons had bought a restaurant.

"A couple of months later, people were lined up outside the restaurant waiting for tables. We gave them free ouzo. I personally took care of all the customers, taking their orders and passing them on to the waiter. At first, we hired one waiter, then three, and eventually, sixteen.

"One day, our father came by, saw the long line, and immediately stepped in behind the bar to help. Bill stopped him and told him not to worry. Next, my father moved toward the kitchen. I stopped him and also told him not to worry. I said, "Just relax. I'll put a pool table in the middle and we'll shoot some pool." He laughed.

"Our business kept getting better and better. There were lines every Friday and Saturday. A month later, there were lines every day."

Chris's many friends in the community came in to help. As business grew, expansion was sorely needed; fortunately, adjacent buildings became available.

CHILDHOOD DAYS AT THE PARTHENON

YANNA SAYS, "WHEN THE PARTHENON opened, I was five years old. I remember quite a bit from those early days, like playing hide-and-go-seek with my brother, Peter, and my cousins, Peter and Petros—Uncle Bill's boys.

Peter, the younger of the two children, adds, "We lived in Norridge, and our mother would take us to The Parthenon occasionally. I was quite excited that my dad owned this restaurant—it was a sense of celebration, as well.

Chris remembers, "We bought the building to the south of The Parthenon in 1971 for $65,000. It took more money and time to fix that side up for the big expansion, which included enlarging the kitchen. The south room gave us an additional 170 seats to add to the original 90 seats.

"During its construction, the new dining room was boarded up to separate it from the main restaurant. There were tables in there, but no decorations on the walls. One night, there was a huge crowd waiting outside, including my dentist! He and his companions told us they'd like us to take the partition down. We did, and Tony Gountanis, now a restaurant and banquet-hall owner, served them in the new, unfinished room. In fact, we filled the new room that evening! Dino, my barber, came in to help us give out free ouzo to the people who were lined up.

"Mike and Gus Couchell were here that night, and saw the lines. After seeing our success, they realized that there were opportunities in Greektown. Soon thereafter, they opened Greek Islands, which remains a popular, thriving restaurant today.

"After Greek Islands, the Roditys Restaurant opened. Its owner at that time, Chris, is a friend of mine. He wanted to call it The Pantheon, but we said that would confuse people because it was too similar to The Parthenon. He and his partner already had the sign, napkins, and menus. Everything was ready for the opening of The Pantheon. Unfortunately, we had to take the matter to court, and the judge agreed they could not use the name Pantheon. The restaurant became Roditys, and remains so today. The food is good there.

"The fifth restaurant in Greektown was the Fisherman, which was owned by an attorney and his wife. They sold it to Nick Varvarigos, who changed the name to Acropolis. Later, the restaurant was bought by Jim Kondos, who hired a Greek architect and builder, Dennis Xenos, to redo the restaurant. It became Santorini, the seafood house that remains there today.

"The current restaurant Pegasus, which offers a roof garden, occupies the location of the former Dianna's Grocery and Restaurant. After the first Dianna's closed in 1974, Dianna Opaa, a nightclub that also offered food, was launched in its place. It closed after about two years. Today, that restaurant is known as Athena."

Architect Dennis Xenos, who designed Santorini, has also done most of the remodeling at The Parthenon. Xenos remarked, "Chris is the reincarnation of Zorba the Greek."

Chris continues, "In late 1977, my current partner and chef, Sotiris Stasinos, took over the kitchen. He had been in charge of making the gyros since 1974, but the head chef, Angelo, liked him and trained him for every position in the kitchen. Several years later, Angelo moved to Greece. Since then, Chef Sotiris has been the head chef—that's almost 31 years now!"

No Midlife Crisis

Chris recalls, "In 1981, I opened Courtyards of Plaka down the street, at the corner of Halsted and Van Buren. Paul Dukas was the designer. It was beautiful—built to resemble the Plaka in Greece, with a piano on stage. The service was upscale, and the food was served on trays instead of by hand, as at The Parthenon. It was a good business, but it became too difficult to run back and forth. I had to be here most of the time, so after several years of juggling both restaurants, I sold Courtyards to its manager, Costa Vlahos. Today, the restaurant still bears his name.

"When we built the new bar in the building to the north in 1996, we were renting the front space. When the *bouzouki* music bar next door closed, we turned that space into a banquet room. The upper floors of both the north and south buildings were renovated into beautiful apartments, and in 1995, I created my own home on the top floor of the main Parthenon building. My roof garden is adjacent to it, on top of the south part of the restaurant building. Eventually, we bought the whole building in 2007."

Chris's private roof garden offers a beautiful view of Chicago's downtown skyline, surrounded by lovely flowers along the garden wall. It's quite a climb, all the way up four floors. There are sixty-six stairs, to be exact, to reach the top. Chris says that he combines all that stair-climbing with swimming to stay fit.

The 21st Century

Chris recalls, "The banquet facility next door, in the north building, was completed in September 2002. It has allowed us to handle large parties and meetings. We can seat approximately 200 people for a sit-down dinner, or 250 for a stand-up reception. The room, which has two bars and a dance floor, is very popular and has really increased our business.

"On July 5, 2003, we celebrated The Parthenon's 35th anniversary in the new facility with a party complete with buffet dinner, live music, dancing and, of course, a big cake for dessert. That time, we even brought in belly dancers for entertainment."

Chris and his wife, Lorraine, return to Greece each year to visit his brothers, Bill and George, and his sister, Chrisoula. He always stops by his hometown as well to visit his boyhood friends. On these trips, Chris says, "I am always looking for something new to inspire me, to incorporate in the restaurant somehow. I'm considering putting salted dried cod on the menu…

A FORMER WAITER RECALLS THE 1970S

ANTONIS (TONY) GOUNTANIS, CHEF AND CO-OWNER OF CHICAGO'S VERANDA Char House and Regency Inn Banquets, remembers his own personal history at The Parthenon: "I arrived at The Parthenon in 1971, right after its first big expansion, and worked there as a waiter until 1974. I really respected Chris and Bill, because I knew what they were trying to do at the restaurant—good quality, fresh food, and excellent service."

Tony continues, "I was the only waiter who ever held 11 flaming saganaki at once!

"When I was working at The Parthenon—this was before credit cards were so prevalent—one of my customers realized that he'd forgotten his wallet, his money. He was upset, but I told him not to worry about it—I paid his bill. The man returned to repay me, and from then on, he always asked for Tony, and he brought many people to join him at the restaurant. That is what Greek *filoxenia* is all about—I love people, and I treat them well.

"At the time, The Parthenon had six gyros machines, and they sold the most gyros in Chicago. Their gyros were the best, and they still are today. The Parthenon is a very traditional, warm, homey restaurant with classic Greek cuisine. It's not commercial, and I respect that.

"Before the 1970s, Greektown had many more nightclubs. The Lawrence and Western Avenues area had more Greek restaurants than Halsted Street did. That has all changed. Greektown has a great location—near the expressways and downtown—and it's easy to get to. Today, it's the best Greektown in the U.S!"

Greek people like it. Now we serve fresh cod, which Americans seem to enjoy. We have different dishes from the north and south of Greece, and we try to offer classic Greek cuisine from all of the country."

In the summer of 2007, wildfires tore through large portions of Greece, causing extensive destruction to homes and businesses and killing many people as well. When I asked Chris about the fires, he said, " It brought tears to my eyes to see the destruction of the villages and the beautiful mountains and trees. The fires nearly destroyed the Olympic Museum. But at the last moment, God changed the winds and blew the fire in the other direction."

GREEKTOWN TODAY

The restaurants and businesses of Greektown grew through the years, but not always consistently. Residents left the neighborhood in the 1980s, and activity diminished a bit. The leaders of the Greek community developed a revitalization and redevelopment plan that took years of work.

REMEMBERING THE PARTHENON—FROM THE INSIDE

Manuel Gonzalez, bartender—31 years of service: "I started as a dishwasher in 1977, when the restaurant was nine years old. I moved on to preparing salads, then became a busboy. I've become a bartender—now in the renovated bar. I've seen The Parthenon grow, with more customers and expansions."

Salvador Martinez, waiter—26 years of service: "I started in the kitchen, helping make salads and cold foods, and stayed there about five years. Later, I moved up front and became a bus boy, helping the waiters. About 12 years ago, I became a waiter. John Sarikas was the manager then; he later became general manager. I see lots of new customers, but I've seen plenty of regulars for all 25 of those years. Their young children are now adults, and many of them are regulars, too. They always ask for Chris, for me, or for John."

Bob Tzanetopoulos, waiter—15 years of service: "A lot has changed in 15 years. When I started in 1993, there weren't so many restaurants in Greektown. Now there are more restaurants and shops, more tourists and people—the whole area is busier now."

As the November 30, 1995 edition of the *Greek Star* reported, the first phase of Chicago's Greektown renovation plans included a grant of $2 million from the city of Chicago. Mayor Richard M. Daley saw the plan, which included the establishment of a permanent Hellenic Museum and Cultural Center, as an important part of his plan to rejuvenate Chicago.

The article stated, "The proposed renovation plan consists of three main phases… The first phase, comprised of a $2 million Chicago city grant, will provide funding for resurfacing streets, extending sidewalks, installing street lighting and traffic signals, and lining Halsted Street, from Van Buren to Madison Streets, with trees."

GreekTown USA spokeperson James Regas was quoted as saying, "This is a project that will raise the identity of the Greek community. I have never seen the city so organized and enthusiastic about something. It is a direct reflection of the mayor's own enthusiasm about this."

The article noted that the project's second phase entailed erecting ornamental Greek columns and monuments at the various Greektown boundaries along Halsted Street. Phase three involved construction of the new Hellenic Museum and Cultural Center, which was to be funded through contributions and assistance from the United Hellenic American Congress. Phase one began on April 1, 1996, and was completed by August 1 of that same year.

In the fall of 2005, a building at 333 S. Halsted Street, across the street from The Parthenon, was demolished to make way for the new Hellenic Museum and Cultural Center; construction of the center will be completed in the near future. Because of the "Sister City" agreement that exists between Athens and Chicago, the museum will be entitled to receive artifacts and temporary exhibits from Athens's Hellenic Museum. Regas remarked, "It will create a cultural center for our thoughts, our ideas, and our heritage."

In particular, Chris highlighted two community events that have been very helpful to Greektown business. The annual Greek Parade used to be on Michigan Avenue, and for several years it has been rerouted to pass through Greektown, bringing many spectators into the area. The Taste of Greece Festival, which is held on the last weekend in August, always attracts many newcomers.

Greektown thrives today, boasting 26 various businesses, most of them Greek-related. On Halsted between Madison to Van Buren, there are 14 Greek restaurants and cafes, including a bakery/café, Artopolis, and the Athens Grocery & Liquor and Pan Hellenic Pastry Shop. There are other stores with a connection to Greece: The Greektown Music Store, the Athenian

Candle Company, and several other businesses serve the community. It is a welcome place for Greeks—and everyone else—to dine; buy gifts, music, and religious items; learn about Greek culture; and enjoy nightlife and music.

A Look Into the Crystal Ball

For four decades, Chris Liakouras has devoted himself to The Parthenon, taking the responsibility for excellence seriously. Now that Yanna and Peter have been managing the restaurant for several years, I asked Chris to tell me whether there are any plans for expansion.

He said, "Yes—we have been talking about opening a second restaurant eventually. Now that my daughter and son are with me, it would be easier."

Yanna added, "For the future, we all [Chris, Peter, Sotiris and I] agree that we want The Parthenon to continue to thrive!

"We would also like to see the completion of the Hellenic Museum, part of the wonderful expansion of Greektown, and the possibility of the Olympic Games coming to Chicago [Chicago is being considered as a host for the 2016 Olympics]… that would be a dream come true!

"We all love and adore the fact that we have generations of families coming here, and we watch them grow and eventually have their own children. The future for us is really now."

CHAPTER THREE
The Recipes

GREEK CUISINE IS OFTEN REFERRED TO AS a Middle Eastern cuisine, but today it is also grouped with the celebrated "Mediterranean diet," which includes cuisines of other countries around the Mediterranean Sea (such as Italy). The Mediterranean's sunny climate grows an abundance of crops, and the sea itself supplies a massive variety of fish and seafood, including sea bass, red snapper, cod, squid, octopus, and shrimp. Traditional Greek preparations include broiling, grilling, baking, braising, and boiling. Some types of seafood (e.g., calamari or squid) are fried quickly in olive oil, resulting in a delightfully crispy, nongreasy dish. Meats, including lamb, pork, chicken, and game birds, also receive healthful preparations, including traditional roasting, rotisserie-roasting, grilling, and braising. Beef rarely appears on Greek menus.

The bountiful harvest of Greece includes a profusion of vegetables, including green beans, eggplant,

No trip to The Parthenon would be complete without an order of Saganaki (flaming cheese), which was invented by founding brothers Bill and Chris Liakouras.

zucchini, broccoli, carrots, okra, green peas, artichokes, and onions, as well as many fresh aromatic herbs—especially dill, oregano, parsley, and garlic. There are dried legumes, as well—a variety of beans are used in salads, soups, and as side dishes. Luscious fruits abound, including ripe tomatoes, figs, grapes, and melons.

Olive oil, the main source of fat in the Greek diet, has been deemed one of the healthiest oils or fats you can use in the kitchen. Many Greek dishes are prepared with olive oil and flavored with olives.

Dairy products include a delicious, thick, velvety yogurt, which is a common base for sauces (tzatziki) and desserts (yogurt with honey and walnuts—a simple and delicious treat). Feta, kefalotiri, and kasseri cheeses are used in many Greek dishes.

Grains, especially rice, are a key accompaniment to Greek entrees, and locally grown wheat is used to prepare fresh Greek breads.

Locally produced honey, walnuts, almonds, and fruit preserves all play important roles on the Greek culinary stage.

Greek wines are produced from reportedly 300-plus native grape varietals grown in Greece's many landscapes and various microclimates. The Greek winemaking tradition is thousands of years old. Many of the local Greek wines perfectly complement the flavorful regional food.

For many years, Greek wine was fairly difficult to find in the United States. The quality of Greek wines improved immensely in the 1990s, and many Greek wines are now imported to the U.S. Basic styles include roditis, a versatile, light, rose-hued wine that pairs with many dishes, and retsina, a resin-based wine that most Greeks enjoy, but can be an acquired taste for others. White and red table wines are available as dry or off-dry, and sweet wines are available as well—something for every taste.

The Parthenon features classic Greek cuisine and some original creations. Its extensive menu lists more than 130 items, and the entire recipe repertoire includes more than 200 dishes. New items are introduced occasionally, and special requests are often filled for private parties and catering orders. In this cookbook, the owners share 50 popular recipes that are relatively easy to reproduce in the home kitchen.

It's best to visit The Parthenon personally to enjoy the rest of its specialties. It will take many visits to sample around the menu. Its wine list is largely Greek, but it does include some options from the United States, Italy, and France.

I am sure you will enjoy discovering the wide variety of healthy choices that Greek cuisine offers. *Kali orexi!* (Good appetite!)

Cold Appetizers

Cold Bean Salad

This substantial salad makes a wonderful appetizer that can join other mezedes to create a light meal, or it can be part of a full vegetarian dinner (see p. 113). Chef Sotiris starts with dried beans to get the firmest texture. For a quick shortcut version, substitute canned beans. When the beans are enhanced with green and red bell peppers, onion, Kalamata olives, dill, and a red wine vinegar and olive oil dressing, they are transformed into a colorful, flavor-rich bean salad you'll be proud to offer on your table. It will most likely become a popular item in your salad repertoire.

YIELD: 6 APPETIZER OR SALAD SERVINGS

2 cups cooked Great Northern beans (see Bean Preparation, below)

1 medium onion, chopped

½ green bell pepper, seeded, chopped

½ red bell pepper, seeded, chopped

½ teaspoon salt

Several grinds of black pepper

½ cup pitted, chopped Kalamata olives

½ cup chopped fresh dill

2 tablespoons red wine vinegar

½ cup extra virgin olive oil

1. In a large bowl, combine all the ingredients and toss well. Add salt and pepper to taste.

2. Cover and refrigerate at least 2 hours.

3. Serve cold.

Bean Preparation

If using canned beans, you'll need 2 (15.5-ounce) cans Great Northern beans. Place in a colander, rinse with tap water, and drain.

If using dried beans, 1 cup dried beans will yield about 2 to 2½ cups cooked beans. Wash beans well, discarding any foreign materials.

Fast soaking method: In a large pot, bring washed beans and 2½ to 3 cups water to a boil. Cover and cook over medium heat about 2 minutes. Remove from heat and let stand, covered, 1 to 1½ hours. Other types of dried beans might require less or more time, depending on size and variety.

Overnight method: Follow the same directions, but allow to stand overnight. If possible, use any residual soaking water, which is full of nutrients, for soup or another use.

COLD OCTOPUS SALAD

This salad is listed as Octopus in Wine and Herbs under Cold Appetizers on the restaurant's menu. The octopus is cooked in white wine with oregano and bay leaves, then cooled, chopped and tossed with celery, onion, basil, or mint. Next, the salad is dressed with a Greek vinaigrette. It's substantial, yet refreshing, and is at home with many other seafood dishes (see Greek Seaside Taverna Menu, p. 113) or as an appetizer at many meals.

YIELD: 4 TO 6 APPETIZER SERVINGS

Octopus:

    5 to 6 baby octopus, fresh or frozen, thawed (about 2 pounds total)

    1 cup dry Greek white wine

    1 tablespoon crumbled, dried oregano

    2 bay leaves

Salad:

    1 small onion, chopped

    2 celery stalks, peeled, chopped

    2 medium leafy, tender stalks fresh basil or mint, finely chopped
       (with the tough stalks discarded)

    ½ cup fresh lemon juice

    ½ teaspoon crumbled, dried oregano

    ⅓ cup extra virgin olive oil

    Salt and ground black pepper, to taste

Garnish: Lettuce leaves, lemon wedges

Optional: Carrot slices, ½ cucumber slices and Kalamata olives

1. Thaw octopus under cold running water if frozen. Place thawed octopus in a large pot over low heat. The octopus will express enough water to finish the cooking process. When the water releases and the octopus begins to cook, add wine, 1 tablespoon oregano, and bay leaves. Cover and continue cooking until octopus is fork-tender, about 1 hour.

2. Remove octopus and place pot in sink under cold running water. When octopus is cool enough to handle, remove from water. Remove the octopus's outer skin (it will slide off easily). Place octopus in bowl, cover, and refrigerate.

3. Once chilled, transfer to cutting board and chop octopus into chunky bite-size pieces.

4. In a medium bowl, combine the onion, celery, and basil. Add the chopped octopus.

5. In another small bowl, add lemon juice and ½ teaspoon oregano and slowly whisk in the olive oil. Add the salt and pepper to taste. Pour over the vegetables and octopus and stir well. Cover and chill.

6. Serve chilled over lettuce with lemon wedges.

MELITZANOSALATA (EGGPLANT SALAD)

Melitzanosalata, or eggplant salad, is served at The Parthenon as a spread with Greek bread. Garlic is a key flavor ingredient here, like many other Greek appetizers and dishes, and it's yet another reason why the Mediterranean diet is so healthful. This appetizer gets its smooth consistency from olive oil, its tang from red wine vinegar, and its fresh taste and texture from parsley (see photo, p. 30).

YIELD: 6 TO 8 APPETIZER SERVINGS*

> 5 medium eggplants
> ½ cup flat-leaf parsley, finely chopped
> 1 garlic clove, finely chopped
> ½ cup olive oil
> ½ cup red wine vinegar
> Greek bread

1. Heat oven to 350°F.

2. Place the whole eggplants in an ovenproof pan; do not cut or chop them. Bake for 1 hour or until very soft, turning over occasionally. Remove from the oven when the eggplants appear to be wilted and soft. Let cool.

3. When cool enough to handle, remove the peel from the eggplants, halve them, and remove the seeds. Chop eggplant and place it in a large bowl. Add chopped parsley and garlic. Stir with a wooden spoon while adding the oil and vinegar. Continue until all the oil and vinegar has been used.

4. Transfer to a clean bowl; let cool. Cover and refrigerate 2 to 3 hours before serving with Greek bread.

*NOTE: The Parthenon's servings are large; this recipe will easily serve 8 to 10 as a side dish.

Melitzanosalata · Tirosalata · Tzatziki Sauce with Pita Bread

SKORDALIA (GREEK POTATOES PURÉED WITH GARLIC)

Skordalia is a spread served as a cold appetizer. It is an excellent accompaniment to Pan-Fried Codfish or Pan-Fried Zucchini (see pp. 38 and 62).

YIELD: ABOUT 1¼ CUPS, 4 TO 5 APPETIZER SERVINGS

4 medium potatoes, boiled, peeled, and quartered

½-¾ teaspoon salt

Several grinds of freshly ground black pepper

4 cloves of garlic, finely chopped

Juice of ½ a fresh medium lemon

1 cup extra virgin olive oil

Chopped parsley

Carrot slices

1. Place potatoes, salt, pepper, garlic, and lemon juice in a medium mixing bowl.

2. Using an electric hand mixer or standard standing mixer set at medium speed, start blending the potato mixture and slowly add a ribbon of olive oil. Continue mixing until the potato mixture is smooth, without lumps. Cover and refrigerate.

3. When ready to serve with fried codfish, serve either on the same platter or in a separate dish. Sprinkle with chopped parsley, and garnish with carrot slices, as desired.

TARAMOSALATA (FISH ROE SALAD)

A prominent feature on the cold appetizer special platter, and also available alone, this fish roe spread, as it is called on The Parthenon menu, is very popular. Serve it with several other appetizers for a light meal, or as the first course of a seafood lunch (see Greek Seaside Taverna Menu, p. 113).

YIELD: 8 APPETIZER SERVINGS

1 pound loaf white bread

1 (10-ounce) jar (about 1 cup) tarama fish roe (carp roe caviar)*

½ teaspoon ground white pepper

½ cup extra virgin olive oil, or slightly more as needed

¼ cup fresh lemon juice

Garnish: Lettuce leaves, half-slices cucumber, carrot slices (crosswise)

Optional garnish: 1 pitted Kalamata olive, quartered lengthwise,
     lemon slices, or tomato slices

Greek bread or pita bread wedges

1. The day before making Taramosalata, store bread in dry area overnight; it should be dry for this recipe.

2. On the following day, using a sharp, serrated knife, cut the crust portion off the loaf. Slice bread into several thick slices. Submerge the crustless white bread in a large bowl of water until thoroughly soaked, about 2 to 3 minutes. Using clean hands, squeeze out the water.

3. Place the wet bread in a food processor bowl. Add the fish roe and the white pepper and blend well on low speed. Increase speed to medium. While mixing, slowly add ½ cup olive oil and the lemon juice. Continue mixing until the fish roe salad has a puréed texture. Add slightly more olive oil if necessary. Consistency should be thick enough to spread.

4. Cover and chill until flavors blend and mixture is cold, about 2 hours or overnight.

5. When ready to serve, shape into a mound onto lettuce-lined salad plate; garnish around the base with cucumber and carrot slices; garnish top with olive quarters, lemon slices, or tomato slices. Serve with Greek or pita bread.

* Carp Roe Caviar is found at Greek groceries.

TIROSALATA (CHEESE SPREAD)

Tirosalata is a protein-rich vegetarian appetizer that gets a punch of flavor impact from the feta, herbs, garlic, and peppers. Serve with crusty bread and other appetizers for a mezedes meal, or make it part of a multi-course Vegetarian Meal (see p. 113).

YIELD: 8 APPETIZER SERVINGS.

    1 pound feta cheese, crumbled*
    ½ pound ricotta cheese
    2 teaspoons chopped fresh dill
    2 teaspoons chopped flat-leaf parsley
    2 tablespoons finely chopped red bell pepper
    2 tablespoons finely chopped green bell pepper
    ½ teaspoon finely chopped garlic
    ½ teaspoon ground white pepper
    3 tablespoons extra virgin olive oil
    Greek bread
    Optional garnish: Lettuce leaves; pitted Kalamata olive, quartered lengthwise;
        several thin slices red bell pepper

1. Rinse the feta cheese with water to remove some of its saltiness. Drain well.

2. Add the crumbled feta and ricotta into a small mixer bowl; mix on medium speed to blend. Add the dill, parsley, red and green bell peppers, garlic, and white pepper; continue mixing.

Slowly add the olive oil. Tirosalata is ready when it has a puréed texture. Cover and chill at least 2 hours or overnight.

3. When ready to serve with Greek bread, line a serving plate with lettuce leaves. Mound the Tirosalata in the center. Garnish with Kalamata olive slices on top and arrange red pepper slices around the base.

* Rinsing the feta well with water removes some saltiness. For those who prefer a less salty finished product, substitute ¼ pound ricotta for ¼ pound feta.

Tzatziki Sauce (Yogurt with Garlic and Cucumber)

This is a very refreshing appetizer, with thick, tart Greek yogurt combined with cucumber and accented with garlic, red wine vinegar, and olive oil. It is also served as a sauce with gyros, The Parthenon's homemade specialty: spit-roasted slices of mixed lamb and beef, served on a bed of sliced onions. It's the perfect complement!

YIELD: 8 APPETIZER SERVINGS

1 pound thick Greek yogurt*
2 cloves garlic, crushed
1 medium cucumber, peeled, seeded, finely chopped
2 tablespoons red wine vinegar
Salt, to taste
Freshly ground black pepper, to taste
¼ cup extra virgin olive oil
Garnish: Lettuce leaves, cucumber slices sprinkled with paprika,
    carrot slices, sprig fresh dill
Greek bread

1. In a large bowl, combine all ingredients with pepper and stir.

2. Gradually add oil while stirring. Add salt and pepper to taste, stirring until well blended.

3. Transfer to a lettuce-lined decorative serving dish, cover and refrigerate for at least 1 hour, or overnight.

4. Taste Tzatziki. If you prefer a stronger garlic flavor, stir in additional crushed garlic, cover, and refrigerate another 3 hours.

5. When ready to serve on lettuce, garnish with cucumber slices, carrot slices, and fresh dill sprig and serve with Greek bread.

*The Parthenon drains its homemade yogurt in order to thicken it.

Hot Appetizers

Keftedes (Broiled Meatballs)

This delicious combination of beef and lamb is seasoned with onion, oregano, garlic, and mint and shaped into meatballs. Make them in whatever size you prefer, but adjust broiling time per recipe. They are satisfying as mezedes, with several other small courses, or as a main course. Roasted potatoes are a wonderful accompaniment. (See Greek Party Menu, p. 116.)

YIELD: 8 TO 10 MEZEDES SERVINGS OR 4 TO 5 MAIN-DISH SERVINGS

2 pounds ground beef

¼ pound ground lamb

1 cup chopped onion

2 tablespoons dried oregano

1 teaspoon salt

½ teaspoon freshly ground black pepper

2 eggs

1 tablespoon chopped garlic

1 cup unseasoned dried breadcrumbs

2 tablespoons chopped fresh mint

Olive oil

Greek Roasted Potatoes (see p. 86)

Garnish: Carrot slices, half lemon slices

1. In a large bowl, combine all ingredients except oil. Mix well, almost kneading the mixture. Cover and refrigerate for ½ hour or more.

2. Form the meat mixture into 8 to 10 smaller meatballs for mezedes servings, or form mixture into 4 to 5 medium meatballs for main-dish servings.

3. Preheat broiler to high.

4. Lightly brush broiler pan with oil. Place meatballs on pan and broil for about 8 minutes for smaller meatballs, 10 minutes for larger meatballs; turn and broil another 8 to 10 minutes on other side.

5. Serve hot with Greek Roasted Potatoes and garnish with carrot slices and half lemon slices.

Spanakotyropita (Spinach-Cheese Pie)

PAN-FRIED ZUCCHINI WITH SKORDALIA

Even finicky eaters would finish their vegetables if they tasted like this! Diagonal slices of zucchini are salted and soaked in cold water to remove excess liquid. They're rinsed, placed in a beer bath, peppered, floured, and fried in olive oil until crispy and golden-brown. Served traditionally with Skordalia (puréed potatoes with garlic), this Greek hot-cold vegetable duet becomes an exciting side dish. It plays a substantial role in the Vegetarian Meal (see menu, p. 113).

YIELD: 6 TO 10 SIDE-DISH SERVINGS

6 medium zucchini, rinsed, cut diagonally (about ¼-inch thick)

Salt, as needed

Cold water, as needed

1 cup beer (lighter-style ale or pilsner)

Freshly ground black pepper

2 cups olive oil

2 to 3 cups flour

Skordalia (see p. 32)

1. Sprinkle zucchini slices well with salt. Place them in a bowl and cover with cold water. Refrigerate for ½ hour.

2. Pour off water; transfer zucchini slices to a colander; rinse very well under cold, running water.

3. Place the zucchini back in the bowl. Pour the beer over and soak zucchini for 5 minutes. Remove zucchini slices from beer marinade; drain. Season zucchini well with pepper.

4. In a large skillet, heat olive oil over high heat. Dredge zucchini slices in flour. Using a long-handled spatula, add several at a time to the hot oil in the skillet until they fill bottom of pan. Fry until golden-brown on both sides, turning as necessary. Zucchini will float to the top when done. Using a slotted spoon, transfer zucchini slices to several layers of paper towels to drain excess oil. Repeat procedure with remaining zucchini slices.

5. Serve zucchini hot with cold Skordalia. When ready to serve Skordalia with Pan-Fried Zucchini, serve either on the same platter or in a separate dish. Sprinkle with chopped parsley, and garnish with carrot slices, as desired.

NOTE: The Parthenon's servings are large; this recipe can easily serve 8 to 10 people.

PAN-FRIED KALAMARI (SQUID)

Fried calamari, or calamari, is often the first introduction that neophytes have to eating squid. If it's crispy outside and delicate inside, it can be so delicious that even youngsters would be willing to try other preparations, such as stuffed squid. However, many versions of fried Kalamari are so rubbery and distasteful that they may cause a novice to avoid squid forever. The Parthenon's delectable Kalamari has won over budding connoisseurs and mature gourmets alike. For those squeamish cooks who can't get used to the idea of cleaning raw squid (also known as inkfish), cleaned whole squid and rings are available frozen.

YIELD: 4 TO 6 MAIN DISH SERVINGS OR 8 APPETIZER SERVINGS

2 pounds raw or frozen, cleaned kalamari, thawed

About 2 cups olive oil

Salt and freshly ground black pepper

About 1 cup flour

Lemon wedges

1. *If using raw kalamari*: To clean each one, pull out the head, and most of the entrails will follow it. Rinse tubular bodies under cold running water. Place tubular body on a cutting board. Cut head below the beak (the hard ball inside the head), reserve tentacles, and discard the rest of the head and ink. Remove the transparent quill and any remaining entrails from the body. Repeat for each squid. Rinse bodies well under cold running water and pat dry; cut into serving pieces. Pat dry.

If using frozen kalamari: Thaw and clean well under cold running water. Some packages contain tubular bodies and tentacles on the side. Arrange squid bodies on a large cutting board, and using a sharp knife, slice into ½-inch thick slices.

2. In a deep skillet, add olive oil until the skillet is half full. Heat oil over medium-high heat until hot, ensuring that it does not smoke or bubble. (Olive oil has a lower smoking point than traditional frying oils.)

3. Transfer the kalamari to a medium bowl; sprinkle well with salt and pepper. Fill a medium-size bowl halfway with flour. Dredge each piece of seasoned kalamari in flour, shake off excess.

4. Place small batches of floured kalamari on slotted spoon and lower into hot oil. Turn kalamari over to cook to golden on all sides. When done, they will float to the top and have a light golden color.

5. Using a large wire basket, strainer spoon or slotted spoon, remove fried kalamari to a pan lined with several layers of paper towels; drain to remove excess oil. Serve hot with lemon wedges.

Saganaki (Melted and Flambéed Cheese Appetizer), an original creation of The Parthenon Restaurant

Saganaki was imported to the United States as a humble Greek appetizer of melted cheese (usually kefalotiri cheese). It took the creative mind of Chris Liakouras to flambé it with brandy. The Parthenon perfected the recipe with the lighter kasseri cheese and trained its waiters to hold several saganaki orders on a towel-draped arm and ignite the appetizers while exclaiming "Opaa"! (See Parthenon Favorites, p. 117.) Customers love to join in the chorus.

YIELD: 4 APPETIZER SERVINGS

½ cup milk

1 egg

1 pound kasseri cheese, sliced ½-inch thick

1 cup flour

Vegetable oil, as needed

2 lemons, halved

Brandy, optional

Greek bread

1. Beat milk and egg together (batter is sufficient for 4 or 5 slices of cheese).

2. Dip each cheese slice in milk mixture and then in flour. Shake off excess flour. Refrigerate 1 to 3 hours.

3. Pour about ¼ inch of oil in frying pan. Heat oil over medium-low heat, making sure the oil is not too hot. Brown slices in hot oil, about 1 minute per side. Remove and place on heated metal steak plates or individual frying pans. Squeeze lemon juice over the cheese. Serve hot with Greek bread.

NOTE: For safety's sake, it is best to not flambé saganaki at home. To experience it flambéed, visit The Parthenon. The waiter pours ½ shot of brandy over each cheese serving and then ignites and serves it, dousing the flame with lemon juice.

Spanakotyropita (Spinach-Cheese Pies)

This classic specialty is a staple at Greek parties (see Greek Party Menu, p. 116), and a "must" for me just about every time I visit The Parthenon. The flavor combination of spinach with feta cheese, fresh dill, and green onions baked in phyllo is difficult to perfect, and the textural contrasts of the soft spinach-cheese mixture and the flaky pastry create another pleasure for the palate. Spanakotyropita gets my vote for one of the best ethnic creations around. The restaurant also offers triangular Mini Spinach-Cheese Pies, totally wrapped in phyllo, as hot appetizers.

YIELD: 6 TO 9 APPETIZER SERVINGS

1 pound phyllo leaves, 12 x 15 inches

5 pounds fresh spinach, coarsely chopped, or 8 (10-ounce) packages frozen chopped spinach, thawed

¾ cup olive oil

About ½ cup (5 to 6) finely chopped green onions

¼ cup (4 ounces) finely chopped fresh dill

½ teaspoon ground black pepper

2 large eggs

2 pounds Greek feta cheese, crumbled

½ cup (¼ pound) butter, melted

1. Allow phyllo leaves to warm to room temperature, according to package directions.

2. *If using fresh spinach*: Wash very well in several rinses of fresh water. Add the spinach to a large pan, cover; place over low heat and simmer until spinach wilts, about 10 minutes, stirring occasionally. Drain spinach. (It is recommended to rinse spinach several times to remove dirt, sand, bugs, etc.) *If using frozen spinach*: Drain thawed spinach well, squeezing out liquid.

3. Add oil to a large skillet and place over medium heat. When oil is hot, sauté the onions until they begin to sizzle. Add the dill and stir. Add the drained spinach and the pepper, and stir over medium heat for about 15 minutes. Remove skillet from heat.

4. In small bowl, beat the 2 eggs and add to the skillet. Add the feta cheese and mix well.

5. Preheat oven to 350°F.

6. Brush a 9 x 13 x 2-inch baking pan lightly with some of the melted butter. Place a leaf of phyllo in bottom of baking pan, so half of the leaf is in the pan and the other half hangs over edge of the pan. Brush top of phyllo leaf with melted butter. Repeat procedure for 4 to 5 layers of phyllo. While working, keep unused phyllo leaves covered with damp paper towels to prevent them from drying out.

7. Spread spinach mixture evenly over phyllo in pan. Cover the spinach-cheese mixture with the portion of phyllo that is hanging over the edge of the pan. Place another 4 leaves of phyllo on top while brushing each leaf with melted butter. Without cutting all the way through, use a sharp knife to cut the top layer on a diagonal; then cut in opposite direction to form about 9 3-inch diamonds.

8. Bake in preheated oven for 30 to 35 minutes, or until the top crust is puffy and golden. Serve hot.

BROILED RED SNAPPER

Main Dishes

Arni Kokkinisto (Braised Lamb)

Braised lamb is a Parthenon favorite offered with a choice of braised potatoes, Rice Pilafi or any vegetable. (Braised Green Beans is the side dish chosen for the Parthenon Favorites menu [see Parthenon Favorites, p. 117].) Arni Kokkinisto is served in large pieces; the shank is especially popular. It is a traditional main course frequently served at special occasion dinners, and it has many variations. The Parthenon's recipe is simmered until fork-tender, and is redolent of nutmeg, bay leaves, garlic, onion, and tomatoes.

YIELD: 4 TO 6 MAIN-COURSE SERVINGS

2 pounds lamb shoulder or leg, cut into large serving pieces

⅓ cup olive oil

1 medium yellow onion (about 1 cup), chopped

1 clove of garlic, finely chopped

3 ounces dry Greek white wine

2 bay leaves

1 teaspoon salt

½ teaspoon pepper

½ teaspoon ground nutmeg

2 medium tomatoes, peeled, seeded, finely chopped

½ cup tomato paste

2 cups water

1. Rinse lamb; pat dry on paper towels. Set aside.

2. In a large pot, heat olive oil over medium heat. Add the onions and garlic; sauté until transparent, about 2 minutes. Add the lamb, stir and sauté until browned on all sides, about 15 minutes.

3. Add the wine, bay leaves, salt, pepper, nutmeg, and chopped tomatoes, stir well. Cover the pot and cook for another 15 minutes.

4. In a small bowl, stir the tomato paste in the water until tomato paste is dissolved. Add to the lamb mixture in the pan, stirring to blend the sauce into the other liquid. Cover the pot and cook over low heat for about 1½ hours, or until the lamb is fork-tender and separates readily from the bone. A meat thermometer inserted into the meat, away from bone or fat, should register 140°F for rare, 150°F for medium-rare, and 160°F for medium. Remove bay leaves and serve hot.

BROILED RED SNAPPER

Broiled whole fresh fish is a specialty at The Parthenon. Depending on availability, customers choose either red snapper or sea bass. Seasoned with a Greek marinade of olive oil, lemon juice, and oregano and served with rice pilafi, this is one of the simple masterpieces of Greek cuisine (see Greek Seaside Taverna Menu, p. 113).

YIELD: 2 SERVINGS

1 whole red snapper (1-2 pounds), cleaned, scaled

¼ cup olive oil

¼ cup fresh lemon juice

1 teaspoon salt per pound of fish

1 teaspoon dried oregano

Garnish: Lettuce, lemon slices, cucumber slices, carrot slices, or tomato slices

1. Wash fish thoroughly in cold water after cleaning. Pat dry with paper towels.

2. Cut a ¼-inch deep slit down the middle of the fish, nearly the entire length of each side. Place fish in a broiler pan.

3. Combine the olive oil, lemon juice, salt, and oregano, stirring well to blend. Pour half of the sauce into a clean bowl for pouring over the cooked fish. Use the other half to baste the raw fish. Brush top side of fish with about half of the basting mixture.

4. Broil approximately 10 inches from heat source for about 10 minutes.

5. Turn fish over and brush with the remaining basting mixture. Broil 6 minutes more, or until fish begins to flake when tested with a fork. Do not overcook.

6. At this stage, when almost completely cooked, remove fish to platter. Let stand 2 minutes so it will continue cooking. Pour remaining reserved oil-lemon juice mixture over fish.

7. Serve on lettuce-lined plate. Garnish with lemon slices, cucumber slices, carrot slices, or tomato wedges.

Chicken Kapama with Rice Pilafi

CHICKEN KAPAMA

Yanna and Chris Liakouras enjoy this home-style chicken dish often. Simmered in tomatoes and white wine with herbs and spices, it has an aromatic note of nutmeg. The house Tomato Sauce is drizzled over the chicken at The Parthenon (see photo, p. 46). The extra sauce is an enhancement, but it's optional for the home cook. The Parthenon serves the dish with rice, potatoes or okra, making it true chicken comfort food.

YIELD: 4 SERVINGS

1 cup olive oil

1 onion, chopped

1 clove of garlic, finely chopped

1 (2 to 3 pound) whole chicken, cut into serving pieces, rinsed, patted dry*

½ cup dry Greek white wine

2 bay leaves

1 teaspoon salt

1 teaspoon pepper

½ teaspoon nutmeg

2 tomatoes, peeled, finely chopped

½ cup tomato paste

2 cups water

Tomato Sauce (recipe follows), optional

1. In a large pot, heat olive oil over medium heat. Sauté onion and garlic until they begin to sizzle.

2. Add chicken pieces and stir for 15 minutes, turning after 7 minutes, until browned on both sides.

3. Add the wine, bay leaves, salt, pepper, nutmeg, and tomatoes and stir. Cover and cook for 15 to 20 minutes.

4. In a small bowl, combine the tomato paste and water, stirring to dilute tomato paste. Pour into the pot with the chicken and stir.

5. Bring to a boil, reduce heat to low, and cover and simmer for about 2 hours; check after 1 hour. If sauce is almost evaporated, add more water. The chicken is cooked when the meat is tender and no longer pink near the bone.

6. Optional: Serve with Tomato Sauce spooned over chicken.

NOTE: The Parthenon serves a generous ½ chicken per serving. This recipe was adjusted to average ½-¾ pound servings, including bones. Instead of a whole chicken, 2 pounds of preferred pieces (light or dark meat) may be substituted.

TOMATO SAUCE

YIELD: ABOUT 1 CUP

3 tablespoons extra virgin olive oil

2 garlic cloves, chopped very fine

1 small onion, chopped very fine

1 cup tomato paste

1 (14.5-ounce) can beef broth (or 3 tablespoons good, thick beef stock)

3 cups water

1 small bunch celery, peeled, finely chopped

¼-½ teaspoon salt

Several grinds of black pepper

1 bay leaf

2 tablespoons sugar

1. In medium saucepan, heat olive oil over medium heat. Add the garlic and onions; sweat vegetables until slightly transparent.

2. Add tomato paste and stir for 1 minute. Add beef broth and water; stir to blend the tomato paste into the liquid.

3. Add remaining ingredients and cook on medium-low heat for about 1 hour, stirring occasionally. Sauce should be rather thin and pourable. If the sauce becomes too thick, add a little more water and heat.

4. Pour the sauce through a strainer. Serve warm.

CHICKEN SOUVLAKI (CHICKEN BREAST SHISH KEBOB)

The Chicken Souvlaki is a favorite among the ten different chicken dishes listed on The Parthenon's menu. It is colorful and succulent, served with roasted potatoes and rice pilaf. It's also easy to prepare at home; the ingredients are marinated in a lemon juice-oregano blend. Then skewer the chicken cubes alternately with green bell peppers, tomatoes, and onions, and broil or grill. The chicken derives moisture from the vegetables as the kebobs cook until they are golden-brown. See Parthenon Favorites (p. 117).

YIELD: 6 SHISH KEBOB MAIN-DISH SERVINGS

6 long (10-inch) metal or wooden skewers

3 pounds chicken breasts, split, skinned, boned, cut into 1¾-inch cubes

1 tablespoon salt

1 tablespoon freshly ground black pepper

1 tablespoon dried oregano

½ cup fresh lemon juice

½ cup (4 ounces) vegetable oil

2 medium green peppers, cored, seeded, cut into thirds

2 medium tomatoes, cut into thirds, seeded

2 medium onions, peeled, cut into thirds

1. If using wooden skewers, soak in water for ½ hour before using.

2. In a large bowl, add the chicken cubes, salt, pepper, oregano, lemon juice, and oil; mix gently. Add green pepper, tomato, and onion pieces to bowl; stir to moisten ingredients. Cover and refrigerate for about 1 hour.

3. When ready to prepare shish kebobs, thread 1 cube of chicken through a skewer, then a piece of green pepper, another cube of chicken, a piece of tomato, another cube of chicken, a piece of onion. Continue alternating chicken, vegetables, and tomato until the shish kebob reaches the desired size. Repeat procedure for remaining ingredients, dividing them evenly among the 6 skewers.

4. Arrange the shish kebobs on the broiler pan, leaving a space between them; place in broiler about 5 inches from heat source. *Broil method*: Broil 8 to 10 minutes, turning after 4 to 5 minutes to cook evenly. Chicken is done when the interior flesh is no longer pink when tested with a sharp knife and the exterior is golden-brown. Avoid overcooking; ingredients will continue to cook after removed from heat. *Grill method*: Arrange shish kebobs on a foil-lined pan; place on grill over medium-hot coals. Cook as above, turning after 4 minutes to cook evenly. Depending on coals, chicken may cook faster on the grill. Test for doneness sooner.

CHICKEN SPANAKI

Chicken Spanaki makes a beautiful presentation—stuffed chicken breasts filled with a luscious spinach-feta filling. Whole chicken breasts are pounded until flattened, so they can be easily filled and fastened shut for broiling. Before they are removed from the broiler, they are moistened with Greek Sauce. The Parthenon serves one stuffed chicken breast with Rice Pilafi per person (see photo, p. 52).

YIELD: 8 STUFFED BREASTS (8 LARGE MAIN-DISH SERVINGS)

8 whole (11 ounces each) boneless, skinless chicken breasts

2 10-ounce packages frozen chopped spinach, thawed

⅓ cup olive oil

½ cup green onion, chopped

1 medium onion, peeled, chopped

½ cup chopped fresh dill

1 pound feta cheese, crumbled

2 medium eggs, beaten

1 tablespoon freshly ground black pepper

Greek Sauce (recipe follows)

1. Place chicken breasts in the center of a plastic food storage bag or 2 large sheets of waxed paper. Pound out the chicken from the center of the bag using a heavy-bottomed skillet or mallet, evenly flattening the breasts until thin enough to stuff and fold.

2. Place the spinach in a large strainer and press out excess liquid.

3. In a large skillet, heat ⅓ cup oil over medium heat. Sauté both the onions for 1 minute. Add the spinach; sauté, stirring occasionally, for about 10 minutes. Transfer to large bowl to cool.

4. When the mixture is cool, add the dill, feta, beaten eggs, and pepper; mix well. Fill each chicken breast with ⅛ of the spinach mixture. Close each breast around the filling and fasten with wooden pick or short skewer.

5. Arrange chicken breasts in a shallow broiler pan. Broil chicken 5 to 6 inches from heat source, about 5 minutes per side. Remove broiler pan; remove picks or skewers and open chicken breasts so insides will cook thoroughly. Return to broiler and broil 5 minutes. Remove broiler pan again, fold chicken breasts around filling and fasten with picks or skewers; turn breasts over. Return to broiler and broil another 5 minutes, or until chicken is done. Interior flesh should not be pink.

6. Before removing chicken from broiler, douse evenly with Greek Sauce. Serve hot.

NOTE: The Parthenon's servings are very generous. This recipe can easily serve 16 average appetites; stuffed breasts would need to be halved, however, and the presentation would not be as attractive.

Chicken Spanaki with Rice Pilafi

GREEK SAUCE

¾ cup olive oil

½ cup lemon juice

1 tablespoon dried oregano

In a small bowl, combine ingredients for Greek Sauce, stirring to blend.

DOLMADES (STUFFED GRAPE LEAVES)

Dolmades *(pronounced Dol-MAH-Thes) is the epitome of Greek cuisine. It blends tart grape leaves, fresh dill, lemon juice, and olive oil, connecting the vineyard, garden, orchard, and olive grove to the table. Chef Sotiris prefers ground beef and short-grain rice, with onion, dill, salt, and pepper as the seasonings, thus streamlining the recipe. There are as many versions as there are chefs and cooks. This one, served with Avgolemono Saltsa, has won raves. The Parthenon also serves Vegetarian* Dolmades, *grape leaves stuffed with rice and herbs, and a cold appetizer version that is stuffed with herbal rice. The singular of* Dolmades *is Dolma.*

YIELD: ABOUT 40 DOLMADES (4 MAIN-DISH SERVINGS OR 10 TO 12 APPETIZER SERVINGS)

1 pound ground beef

1 cup short-grain rice (not instant)

½ cup milk

1 medium onion, finely chopped

3 eggs

½ cup finely chopped dill

¼ cup fresh lemon juice, divided

¼ teaspoon salt, or to taste

⅛ teaspoon freshly ground black pepper, or to taste

50 large grape leaves (usually packed in salt brine in 12-ounce jars, found at Greek markets)

About 2 tablespoons olive oil

About 1 quart water, or more as needed

Avgolemono Saltsa (Egg-Lemon Sauce) (recipe follows)

1. Mix together beef, rice, milk, onion, eggs, dill, and half of the lemon juice. Season with salt and pepper to taste. Set aside.

2. Remove stems from grape leaves. Any tough stems that have grown into the leaf may be carefully cut out with a sharp knife. Soak leaves in tepid water for 30 minutes. Remove leaves from the water and rinse well. Sort and set aside any leaves that are too small, tough, or torn;

reserve rejects for lining bottom of pan. Stack the good leaves with the dark, shiny sides down and their pointed tops all in the same direction to make the filling process more efficient.

3. Working with one leaf at a time, lay each leaf down with the top middle peak pointing up and away from you. Place a tablespoon of meat mixture near the bottom of each leaf, leaving a small border from the edge; fold the stem end up, then the sides in over the filling, and roll the leaf away from you until it becomes a sealed roll. Make sure filling is encased to avoid leakage during cooking, but avoid wrapping the rolls very tightly, since the rice expands during cooking. If a leaf tears, select another and transfer the filling; reserve the torn leaf and any others for lining the bottom of the pot in which the Dolmades will cook.

4. Coat the bottom of a deep pot (6- to 8-quart) with olive oil. Line the bottom of the pot with the reserved and remaining grape leaves. Place the stuffed grape leaves in a tight arrangement on top of the grape leaves lining the bottom of the pot, making as many layers as necessary.

5. Combine 1 quart water with remaining 2 tablespoons lemon juice; pour into pot until the liquid is about 2 inches above the level of the Dolmades. Place a heavy, heat-proof plate or any round, heavy pan on top of the Dolmades to prevent them from floating in the liquid. Bring to a boil over medium-high heat, reduce heat to low, cover, and simmer for about 1½ hours. Halfway through cooking, add more water if necessary.

6. Remove from heat. Drain liquid into a separate bowl and reserve 2 cups of the Dolmades stock for the Avgolemono Saltsa. Keep Dolmades covered and warm. Prepare Avgolemono Saltsa.

7. Remove the Dolmades from the pot and place them on a large platter or arrange on individual plates. Pour the Avgolemono Saltsa over them.

AVGOLEMONO SALTSA (EGG-LEMON SAUCE)

YIELD: ABOUT 2¾ CUPS

3 eggs, separated, at room temperature
¼ cup fresh lemon juice
2 tablespoons cornstarch
2 cups of the reserved stock from the Dolmades

1. In a small mixing bowl at medium mixer speed, beat egg whites until white and frothy, like a meringue. Whisk egg yolks in a separate small bowl until light in color. Continue beating egg whites while gradually adding the yolks; then add the lemon juice and the cornstarch, one at a time.

2. Vigorously beat the egg mixture while slowly adding one ladle of the stock at a time, continuing until all is incorporated.

3. Pour the sauce into a pan and keep warm over low heat. Serve warm with Dolmades.

Greek Meat Sauce with Spaghetti

The scent of cloves infused with oregano, bay leaves, and onion transforms this spaghetti meat sauce into a specialty. This magical combination of several ingredients elevates a common item to a main dish fit for guests. With or without cheese on top, Greek Meat Sauce with Spaghetti is hearty and delicious (see Parthenon Favorites, p. 117).

YIELD: 4 TO 6 MAIN-DISH SERVINGS

½ cup olive oil, plus 2 tablespoons, divided

1 medium onion, chopped

2 pounds ground beef

1 medium tomato, chopped

2 tablespoons tomato paste diluted in 1 cup water

1 teaspoon salt

½ teaspoon ground black pepper

2 bay leaves

3 to 4 cloves

½ cup dry white Greek wine

1 teaspoon sugar

½ teaspoon dried oregano

1 (1-pound) package of spaghetti

2 tablespoons butter, melted

Garnish: ½ pound grated kefalotiri cheese, optional

1. In a large skillet, heat olive oil over medium-high heat. Add onion and cook until translucent.

2. Add beef; stir until browned and crumbled. Drain the fat and oil.

3. Add remaining ingredients through oregano. Bring to a boil, reduce heat to medium-low, and simmer for about 45 minutes. Stir occasionally. If sauce gets thick, add some water. Remove bay leaves. Season with more salt and pepper to taste if necessary.

4. Cook spaghetti according to package directions. Drain. Toss with 2 tablespoons of the reserved olive oil and the melted butter.

5. Toss spaghetti with meat sauce.

6. Optional: sprinkle with kefalotiri cheese.

ROAST LEG OF LAMB

Lamb is the mainstay meat of Greek cuisine, and roast leg of lamb is one of the most popular options. There are many other preparations as well—barbecued lamb and lamb with artichokes, to name two —but this roast leg of lamb is one of the most popular menu items at The Parthenon (see Traditional Greek Meal, p. 112). Some butcher shops will sell boneless leg of lamb, which is easier to carve. However, cooking lamb (or any meat) on the bone yields more flavor. The time of cooking may vary a bit if you substitute a boneless leg. Always use a meat thermometer to determine when the meat is done.

YIELD: 4 MAIN-DISH SERVINGS

1 small leg of lamb (about 3 pounds with bone)

2 teaspoons salt, divided

1 teaspoon pepper, divided

2 teaspoons dried oregano, divided

1 cup fresh lemon juice, divided

½ stick butter, melted, divided

½ cup olive oil, divided

4½ cups water, divided

2 teaspoons cornstarch

1. Preheat oven to 400°F.

2. Wash the lamb well. Place the lamb in a 9 x 13-inch roasting or pan. Season the lamb with half of the salt, half of the pepper, half of the oregano, half of the lemon juice, half of the butter and half of the olive oil. Turn the lamb over and season it with the remaining salt, pepper, oregano, lemon juice, butter, and olive oil. Place the lamb, fat-side up, on pan; place in the preheated oven. Roast for 1½ hours.

3. Turn the lamb over after the fat side turns brown. Add 4 cups of the water to the pan.

4. When the lamb finishes cooking, turn the fat side up and cook for a few more minutes, until browned. Remove lamb from oven. A meat thermometer inserted away from bone or fat should register 140°F for rare, 150°F for medum-rare, and 160°F for medium. Allow roast to stand 5 minutes before carving.

5. To make the gravy, strain the juice into a small pan. Dissolve the cornstarch into remaining ½ cup water and add it to the juice. Heat over medium heat until mixture comes to a boil. Cook, stirring up to 1 minute to thicken. Do not cook longer, or mixture will begin to thin. Serve with sliced lamb.

MOUSSAKA

Eggplant is essential to Italian, French, Greek, and all other Middle Eastern cuisines. It is prepared in various ways: stuffed with meats, cheese, and dried fruits; roasted and mashed for spreads and dips; sautéed; and sliced, layered with other ingredients, and baked. One of these preparations is delicious Greek Moussaka. Yanna says that the purple-black Greek eggplants tend to have bitter juices, so are often sliced, salted, and laid out in the sun for three hours to release the juices. The eggplant is then drained and dried before cooking. Here, we suggest a simpler preparation: an hour-long salt-water bath.

This classic "architectural" creation is built on a foundation layer of eggplant in a kefalotiri cheese-coated baking pan, then a layer of the herbed, spiced beef-lamb-tomato sauce. Layering is repeated, ending with eggplant and a Béchamel Sauce "roof." Baking it releases heavenly aromas of meat, onion, tomatoes, oregano, and sweet allspice and cinnamon. You'll think it came straight from the ancient Greek gods (See Greek Party Menu, p. 116).

YIELD: 6 TO 8 MAIN-DISH SERVINGS

3 medium eggplants, sliced lengthwise, ¼-inch thick

Salted water, as needed

2½ cups plus 3 tablespoons olive oil, divided

1 pound kefalotiri cheese, grated

1 pound ground beef

½ pound ground lamb

1 medium onion, finely chopped

½ cup dry white Greek wine

3 tomatoes, finely chopped

1 tablespoon tomato paste

1 teaspoon dried oregano

3 bay leaves

¼ teaspoon ground allspice

¼ teaspoon ground cinnamon

Salt and freshly ground black pepper to taste

Béchamel Sauce (recipe follows)

Tomato Sauce (see p. 49)

1. Soak eggplant slices in cool, salted water for 1 hour to remove bitter juices. (Smaller, younger eggplants are usually sweeter and require less soaking time.) Remove eggplant and pat dry on several layers of paper towels.

2. In a large sauté pan, heat 2½ cups of the olive oil over medium-high heat. Sauté the eggplant until golden brown. Remove from pan and drain on paper towels.

3. Preheat oven to 325°F.

4. In a large skillet, heat 1 tablespoon of the remaining olive oil over medium-high heat. Cook the ground meats until browned. Drain fat. Add the onion and cook for about 4 minutes. Add the wine and cook for an additional 5 minutes. Add the tomatoes, tomato paste, herbs, and spices and cook for another 15 minutes, stirring occasionally. Let cool. Remove bay leaves. Season with salt and pepper to taste.

5. Prepare Béchamel Sauce.

6. Coat a 9 x 13-inch baking pan with remaining 2 tablespoons of olive oil. Sprinkle with ⅓ of the grated kefalotiri cheese. Arrange a layer of the sliced eggplant and half of the meat mixture. Sprinkle with 2 tablespoons of kefalotiri cheese. Repeat another layer of the eggplant, meat, and cheese. Add another layer of eggplant. Pour the Béchamel Sauce evenly over the meat and eggplant mixture, covering all areas. Sprinkle remaining cheese on top.

7. Bake for 30 to 45 minutes, until golden brown.

8. Cut into 6 to 8 even slices; serve with Tomato Sauce.

BÉCHAMEL SAUCE

YIELD: ABOUT 3½ CUPS SAUCE

2 cups milk
½ pound butter
½ cup cornstarch
1 teaspoon ground nutmeg
½ pound kefalotiri cheese, grated
2 eggs, at room temperature
Salt and ground white pepper, to taste

1. Scald the milk in a small saucepan.

2. In another saucepan, melt the butter, stirring continuously; gradually add the cornstarch, scalded milk, and nutmeg. The sauce should be the consistency of mashed potatoes as you stir; if it gets thicker, add some water. Add cheese and stir to combine. Remove from heat; let cool.

3. Place eggs in a small bowl and whisk or beat with mixer to blend. Stir eggs into the cooled sauce mixture. Season with salt and pepper.

NOTE: Béchamel Sauce is used to top Moussaka (meat or vegetarian) and Pastitsio (meat or vegetarian).

PASTA TOURKOLIMANO

PAN-FRIED CODFISH WITH SKORDALIA

This simple codfish preparation is served with Skordalia (see p. 32), a popular Greek garlic sauce. Prepare it before cooking the codfish. Uninitiated diners might wonder, "Where's the garlic sauce?" when they're served a plate of cold mashed potatoes. That is the Greek Skordalia! Listed under Cold Appetizers on The Parthenon's menu, it is described as "puréed potatoes and intense garlic." (It's intense because raw garlic is added to the cooked mashed potatoes.) After chilling, the flavors meld and the garlic infuses the potatoes. Enjoy Skordalia with Greek bread and other appetizers, or as a traditional partner to this hot codfish dish (see Greek Seaside Taverna Menu, p. 113). Don't try heating Skordalia: The amount of olive oil in it can burn your mouth. Make certain your dining companions all taste Skordalia, too, or be sure to eat some after-dinner breath mints!

YIELD: 4 MAIN-DISH SERVINGS

Skordalia (see p. 32)*
4 frozen fillets of Icelandic codfish, thawed according to package instructions
½ teaspoon salt
½ teaspoon freshly ground black pepper
Olive oil, as needed
2 cups flour
2 lemons, sliced

1. Sprinkle both sides of fillets with salt and pepper.

2. Fill a large, deep skillet with olive oil about ¾ of the way up; heat oil over medium-high heat, being careful not to overheat oil until smoking.

3. Place flour in a deep dish and keep it by the stove. Dredge each piece of codfish in flour, place it on a long-handled slotted spoon, and carefully lower it into the hot oil. Using two long-handled forks or the long-handled slotted spoon, turn the fillets over to ensure they are cooked to golden brown on both sides. When fillets are done, they will float to the top and have a light golden color. Drain well on several layers of paper towels.

4. Serve hot, with chilled Skordalia and lemons on the side.

* When ready to serve Skordalia with codfish, serve either on the same platter or in a separate dish. Sprinkle with chopped parsley, and garnish with carrot slices, as desired.

Pasta Tourkolimano

Tourkolimano is part of Piraeus, the port of Athens, which is very famous for its seafood tavernas. The literal translation of Tourkolimano is "Turkish harbor," for the area where Greeks arrived upon their exodus from Asia Minor, which included most of Asiatic Turkey. This is a stunning dish with exceptional flavor, and it always attracts attention when served at The Parthenon. Large shrimp are the star features here, rimming a plate of spaghetti and a colorful tomato-feta sauce. The delicious tomato sauce is prepared with sautéed red and green bell peppers, a jalapeño pepper, onions, and garlic. It is enhanced with wine, chopped tomatoes, diluted tomato paste, a bay leaf, the flavorful shrimp-boil liquid, mint, and parsley. Crumbled feta is melted in as the final touch. Pasta Tourkolimano makes one guarantee: It brings compliments for the cook.

YIELD: 4 MAIN-DISH SERVINGS

1 (1-pound) package spaghetti

Salted boiling water

6 tablespoons butter, plus ¼ cup for melting

1 quart water

20 large raw shrimp in the shell, deveined, headless

1 cup olive oil

2 large red peppers, seeded, chopped

2 large green peppers, seeded, chopped

2 onions, chopped

2 green onions, chopped

1 jalapeno pepper, seeded, chopped

2 tablespoons chopped garlic

1 cup dry white Greek wine

2 plum tomatoes, chopped

¼ cup tomato paste, diluted in ½ cup water

3 bay leaves

2 teaspoons sugar

1 teaspoon salt

¾ teaspoon freshly ground black pepper

2 tablespoons cornstarch diluted in ¼ cup water

½ cup chopped fresh mint

½ cup chopped Italian parsley, divided

½ pound crumbled feta cheese

1. Prepare spaghetti in salted boiling water according to package directions. Toss spaghetti with 6 tablespoons butter in a pot on very low heat to keep warm.

2. In a medium pot, bring water to a boil; add shrimp. Cook 4 minutes. Remove shrimp and set aside to cool; then peel. Reserve liquid.

3. In a large pot, heat oil over medium-high heat. Add peppers, onions, green onions, jalapeno pepper, and garlic. Cook until soft.

4. Add the wine and chopped tomatoes; cook for 5 minutes.

5. Add diluted tomato paste, shrimp-boil liquid, bay leaves, sugar, salt, and pepper. Bring to a boil, reduce heat to medium-low, and simmer for 45 minutes.

6. Remove from heat and cool slightly. Remove bay leaves. Add diluted cornstarch and stir well. Stir in mint and ½ of the parsley; set aside.

7. In a large pan, melt ¼ cup butter over medium heat. Sauté shrimp. Stir in tomato-vegetable mixture and feta cheese gently and cook for 3 minutes, until cheese is slightly melted. Remove from heat.

8. To serve, place spaghetti on a large serving platter and arrange shrimp around the rim of the platter. Pour tomato-vegetable-feta sauce mixture in center on top of spaghetti. Top with remaining parsley.

THE PARTHENON'S PASTITSIO

Pastitsio is another Greek specialty with many variations. Different cheeses, seasonings, and meats are used. The Parthenon's recipe calls for beef and lamb, kefalotiri cheese, and macaroni #2, which can be found in most Greek markets. Onion, tomato, oregano, allspice, and nutmeg contribute flavors and aromas to the finished baked dish. The Béchamel Sauce adds a creamy texture to this hot main dish, which is very popular (see Combination Plate, p. 116).

YIELD: 6 TO 8 SERVINGS

1 package macaroni #2 (found at Greek markets)*

1 pound kefalotiri cheese, grated, divided

2 eggs, beaten

½ pound butter, cut into small pieces and softened

¼ teaspoon ground nutmeg

6 to 8 tablespoons olive oil, divided

1 pound ground beef

1 pound ground lamb

1 medium onion, finely chopped

½ cup dry white Greek wine
3 tomatoes, finely chopped
1 tablespoon tomato paste
1 teaspoon dried oregano
¼ teaspoon ground allspice
Salt and pepper to taste
Béchamel Sauce (see p. 59)
Tomato Sauce (see p. 49), optional

1. Cook macaroni according to package instructions.

2. In a mixing bowl, combine the macaroni with half the cheese and the eggs, butter, and nutmeg. With clean hands, mix well, making sure all the macaroni is coated with cheese and egg mixture.

3. In a large skillet, heat about 6 tablespoons of olive oil over medium-high heat. Cook the ground meats until browned. Drain fat. Add the onion and cook for about 4 minutes. Add the wine and cook for an additional 5 minutes. Add the tomatoes, tomato paste, oregano, and allspice and cook for another 15 minutes. Let cool. Season with salt and pepper to taste.

4. Preheat oven to 350°F.

5. In a large bowl, combine the macaroni mixture and meat sauce. Using your clean hands, mix the macaroni mixture and meat sauce together.

6. Coat a 9 x 13-inch baking dish with remaining 2 tablespoons of olive oil and sprinkle evenly with ⅓ of the remaining grated cheese. Pour in the macaroni and meat mixture. Evenly sprinkle another ⅓ of the remaining cheese on top.

7. Bake for 15 to 20 minutes. Remove and cool dish. Reduce oven temperature to 325°F.

8. Prepare Béchamel Sauce (see p. 59).

9. Pour Béchamel Sauce evenly over the macaroni and meat mixture. Sprinkle remaining cheese evenly over top.

10. Bake for 30 to 45 minutes, until golden brown. Optional: Serve with Tomato Sauce on the side.

* Ziti pasta may be substituted. Follow package directions.

NOTE: Béchamel Sauce is used to top both Moussaka (meat or vegetarian) and Pastitsio (meat or vegetarian).

CLOCKWISE FROM TOP LEFT: PASTITSIO · GREEK ROASTED POTATOES
MOUSSAKA · BRAISED GREEN BEANS · DOLMA · ROAST LEG OF LAMB

PORK SOUVLAKI (PORK SHISH KEBOB)

The Greek word souvlaki *means shish kebob, and in Greece, lamb, pork, chicken, and swordfish are popular choices for the skewers. Since The Parthenon has such an extensive lamb repertoire, it does not serve lamb shish kebobs, but its pork version is wonderful. About three hours before cooking the kebobs, the pork tenderloin is cubed, seasoned with oregano, salt, and pepper, and marinated in an olive oil–lemon juice–white wine mixture. Pork cubes are then threaded on skewers alternately with tomato, onion, and green pepper before broiling or grilling until golden brown.*

YIELD: 4 SOUVLAKI MAIN-DISH SERVINGS

4 long (10-inch) metal or wooden skewers

4 pounds pork tenderloin, cleaned, trimmed, cut into 1¾-inch cubes

3 tablespoons salt

1½ teaspoons freshly ground black pepper

2 tablespoons dried oregano

¼ cup olive oil

3 to 4 tablespoons fresh lemon juice

½ cup dry white Greek wine

1 large tomato, cut into 8 even pieces, seeded

½ medium onion, peeled, quartered

1 medium green pepper, cored, seeded, quartered

1. If using wooden skewers, soak in water for ½ hour before using.

2. In a large bowl, add pork cubes, salt, pepper, and oregano. Toss with olive oil, lemon juice, and wine, mixing well. Cover; refrigerate mixture for about 2 to 3 hours.

3. When ready to prepare shish kebobs, remove meat and discard marinade. Thread a meat cube onto a skewer, then a piece of tomato, another piece of meat, a piece of onion, another piece of meat, a piece of green pepper, another piece of meat, and another piece of tomato. Repeat process with remaining skewers and ingredients, alternating the meat with vegetables and tomato.

4. Arrange the shish kebobs on the broiler pan, leaving a space between them; place in broiler about 5 inches from heat source. *Broil method*: Broil 8 to 10 minutes, turning after 4 to 5 minutes to cook evenly. Pork is done when the interior flesh is no longer pink when tested with a sharp knife, and the exterior is golden brown. Avoid overcooking; ingredients will continue to cook after removed from heat. *Grill method*: Arrange shish kebobs on a foil-lined pan; place on grill over medium-hot coals; cook as above, turning after 4 minutes to cook evenly. Depending on coals, pork may cook faster on the grill. Test for doneness sooner.

STUFFED SQUID

One of our recipe testers, Sandy, reported that this recipe required a bit more expertise than the Baklava or Octopus Salad she tested. It is a production, but well worth it if you have an adventurous spirit. It's fun to have a friend who likes to cook help you prepare it. (If your friend is squeamish about handling whole squid, don't bother!) If you've tried this deep-flavored, rich textured stuffed squid at The Parthenon, you'll probably be ready to try it at home yourself! (See Greek Seaside Taverna Menu, p. 113.)

YIELD: 6 SERVINGS OF ABOUT 6 STUFFED SQUID EACH, OR ABOUT 12 APPETIZER PORTIONS OF ABOUT 3 EACH

2 cups Tomato Sauce (see p. 49)

1 (40–ounce) package frozen, cleaned kalamari tubes, thawed, rinsed
    (about 1 cup tentacles in package; use ½ cup for recipe)*

½ cup extra virgin olive oil plus 1 tablespoon, divided

1 small onion, chopped

1 bunch green onions, chopped

2 pounds or 3 (10-ounce) packages fresh spinach, rinsed well several times

½ cup chopped fresh dill

½ cup chopped parsley

½ teaspoon each salt and freshly ground pepper, or to taste

½ cup uncooked rice, rinsed

½ cup pine nuts

1 cup chopped tomato

3 tablespoons tomato paste diluted in 2 cups water

½ pound feta cheese, crumbled

1. Prepare a double recipe of Tomato Sauce; set aside.

2. Thaw and rinse the squid bodies, place in a bowl and refrigerate. Rinse and chop about ½ cup of the tentacles. Freeze remaining tentacles for another time.

3. In a large saucepan or pot, heat ½ cup of olive oil. Add chopped tentacles and onions and stir; sauté until onions are translucent, about 6 to 8 minutes. Add spinach, dill, parsley, salt, pepper, rice, and pine nuts. (You may have to add the spinach to the pot in batches and let it cook down.) Wilt spinach mixture, then add chopped tomato and diluted tomato paste. Bring to boil, reduce heat, and simmer for 30 to 45 minutes.

4. Remove from heat. Let cool. Drain well. Once cooled, stir in crumbled feta, mixing well.

5. Preheat oven to 350°F.

6. Brush a 13 x 9-inch baking pan with ½ tablespoon of the remaining olive oil. Put about ½ to 1 cup of the Tomato Sauce in the baking pan to cover the bottom. Stuff kalamari with spinach mixture. Arrange stuffed kalamari tightly in prepared baking pan. Drizzle remaining olive oil and spoon Tomato Sauce over. Bake in 350°F oven for 15 to 20 minutes or until heated through.

* The Parthenon uses large squid; most frozen packages for consumers contain smaller squid.

NOTE: Use a brand-name canned tomato paste.

SWORDFISH SOUVLAKI (SWORDFISH SHISH KEBOB)

Seafood is the largest main-course section of The Parthenon's menu, and swordfish appears twice — swordfish steak and shish kebob, both of which are served with Lemon-Butter Sauce and Rice Pilafi. Shish kebobs are colorful and the fish absorbs juices from the peppers, tomatoes, and onions as they cook. They also may be served with grilled carrots, cauliflower, and broccoli, or any other vegetables you like.

YIELD: 6 MAIN-DISH SERVINGS

6 to 8 (10-inch-long) metal or wooden skewers*

2 pounds swordfish, skinned, cut into 1½-inch cubes

2 teaspoons each salt and ground black pepper, or to taste

1 tablespoon dried oregano

½ cup fresh lemon juice

1 medium green bell pepper, cored, quartered, seeded

1 medium tomato, quartered, seeded

1 medium yellow onion, peeled, quartered

½ cup vegetable oil

Lemon-Butter Sauce (recipe follows)

1. If using wooden skewers, soak in water for ½ hour before using.

2. In a large bowl, add the swordfish, salt, pepper, oregano, and lemon juice and stir to combine. Add the green pepper, tomato, and onion pieces to the swordfish; mix well. Cover, let stand for about ½ hour, or refrigerate for 2 to 3 hours, turning occasionally. Remove from marinade; drain fish, green pepper, tomato, and onion. Discard marinade.

3. To make each shish kebob, place 1 cube of swordfish through the skewer, then a piece of green pepper, a cube of swordfish, a piece of tomato, a cube of swordfish, a piece of onion, and so on until each shish kebob is the desired size. Repeat with remaining swordfish and vegetables until shish kebobs are relatively even in size.

4. Arrange the shish kebobs on the broiler pan, leaving a space between them; place in broiler about 5 inches from heat source. *Broil method*: Broil for 8 to 9 minutes, turning after 4 minutes to cook evenly. Swordfish is done when juices bubble up and the center is almost opaque when tested with a sharp knife. Avoid overcooking; fish will continue to cook after removed from heat. *Grill method*: Arrange shish kebobs on a foil-lined pan; place on grill over medium-hot coals; cook as above, turning after 3 to 4 minutes to cook evenly. Depending on coals, fish may cook faster on the grill. Test for doneness sooner.

5. Serve shish kebobs hot, with Lemon-Butter Sauce on the side.

LEMON-BUTTER SAUCE

½ cup melted unsalted butter
2 to 2½ tablespoons fresh lemon juice
½ to ¾ teaspoon dried oregano, according to taste

Blend melted butter and lemon juice together in small pan; add ½ to ¾ teaspoon oregano. Heat gently.

TIGANIA

Yanna explains that Tigania *is any meat that is thinly sliced and fried. (*Tigani *is the Greek word for frying pan.) In Greece, it is usually served as an appetizer, but The Parthenon created its own unique version as a main course. Pork tenderloin is sliced into thin medallions, marinated in a white wine-olive oil bath, and sautéed in a white wine-tomato sauce. Pork is a light meat that is compatible with both white and light red wines. This is a popular dish that has been on The Parthenon's menu for many years (see Parthenon Favorites, p. 116). The menu suggests serving it with Rice Pilafi and Braised Okra; however, at home you can add any side dishes you prefer.*

YIELD: 4 TO 6 MAIN DISH SERVINGS

2 pounds pork tenderloin, sliced into thin medallions

1 teaspoon salt

¾ teaspoon ground pepper

1 teaspoon dried oregano

1 cup dry white Greek wine, divided

1 cup olive oil, divided

2 tablespoons flour

½ cup Tomato Sauce (see p. 49)

Chopped parsley

1. Season the pork medallions with salt, pepper, oregano, ½ cup of the wine, and ½ cup of the olive oil. Cover and marinate in the refrigerator for 2 hours.

2. Drain the pork. Discard marinade. In a large skillet, heat the remaining olive oil over medium heat. Add enough pork to fill bottom of skillet; cook until browned on both sides. Remove and drain on paper towels. Repeat process until all pork is cooked.

3. Remove pan from heat. Remove the last batch of cooked pork and oil from the pan.

4. Stir in the remaining ½ cup wine and the flour, and place the pan back on the burner. Cook for 2 to 3 minutes, stirring until thickened. Add the Tomato Sauce.

5. Place the pork back into the pan with the Tomato Sauce and mix well. Serve hot, garnished with chopped parsley. Recommended with Rice Pilafi and Braised Okra (see pp. 87 and 85).

VEGETARIAN MOUSSAKA

This hearty vegetarian rendition of Moussaka layers sautéed slices of eggplant with potatoes, zucchini, garlic, parsley, and kefalotiri cheese, then tops it with Béchamel Sauce and more cheese. This culinary creation bakes until heated throughout to meld the flavors and textures, and until it's golden brown on top (see Vegetarian Meal, p. 113).

YIELD: 6 TO 8 MAIN-DISH SERVINGS

2 medium eggplants, trimmed, cut in ¼-inch slices

Salted water

About 2 cups oil, divided

½ medium head garlic, about 5 cloves, finely chopped

2 medium red potatoes, cut in ¼-inch slices

4 medium zucchini, cut in ¼-inch slices

1½ cups grated kefalotiri cheese, divided

½ cup chopped fresh flat-leaf parsley

Béchamel Sauce (see p. 59)

1. Place eggplant slices in cool salted water for ½ to 1 hour to remove bitter juices. (Smaller, younger eggplants are usually sweeter and require less soaking time.) Remove and pat dry.

2. Heat 1 cup of the oil in a large skillet over medium-high heat. First, sauté the garlic until golden; remove and drain on paper towels. Next, sauté eggplant slices on both sides until golden-brown; remove and drain on several layers of paper towels. Sauté the potatoes, then the zucchini, separately, until golden-brown, then remove and drain.

3. Preheat oven to 325°F.

4. Measure ½ cup of the kefalotiri cheese to sprinkle on the bottom of pan; reserve rest for the middle and top. Spray a 12 x 12-inch, or 9 x 13-inch, baking pan, with non-stick spray. Sprinkle the ½ cup kefalotiri cheese over bottom of baking pan.

5. Over the cheese, place a layer of the sliced potatoes, the garlic, and the parsley, then a layer of zucchini, and a layer of eggplant; sprinkle with ½ cup kefalotiri cheese

6. Using a rubber spatula, spread the Béchamel Sauce evenly over the layered vegetables to cover all areas. Sprinkle the remaining ½ cup kefalotiri cheese over the top.

7. Bake in preheated 325°F oven for 30 to 35 minutes, until the top of the sauce turns golden-brown. Remove from oven; let stand 5 minutes before slicing.

TOP LEFT: PAN-FRIED ZUCCHINI

BOTTOM, CLOCKWISE FROM LEFT: VEGETARIAN PASTITSIO

RICE PILAFI · VEGETARIAN MOUSSAKA · BRAISED OKRA

THE PARTHENON'S VEGETARIAN PASTITSIO

This vegetarian version is very different from traditional meat Pastitsio. Ziti pasta is used instead of macaroni #2. Both use eggs and cheese, but they use different cheeses, and both are baked with Béchamel Sauce. The similarities end there. Broccoli, spinach, dill, feta, and kasseri contribute their distinctive flavors to the ziti, eggs, and butter, forming a delectable main dish made all the more satisfying by its crowning glory—Béchamel Sauce (see Vegetarian Meal, p. 113).

YIELD: 6 TO 8 MAIN-DISH SERVINGS

1 pound ziti (macaroni pasta)

2 tablespoons olive oil

Water (per frozen broccoli and spinach package directions)

1 (10-ounce) package chopped frozen broccoli

1 (10-ounce) package chopped frozen spinach

1 pound kasseri cheese, grated, divided

1 pound feta cheese, crumbled

4 medium eggs, beaten

¼ cup finely chopped fresh dill

¼ pound unsalted butter, melted

Salt and freshly ground black pepper, to taste

Béchamel Sauce (see p. 59)

1. Preheat oven to 350°F.

2. In a large pot, boil macaroni according to package instructions; drain, return to pasta pot, toss with olive oil to prevent sticking, and set aside.

3. Bring water to boil in a medium pot over high heat. Briefly plunge frozen broccoli and spinach in hot water for 2 minutes; drain. Transfer to cold water; drain.

4. Spray a 12 x 12-inch or 9 x 13-inch baking pan with non-stick spray. Sprinkle ½ cup of the grated kasseri cheese over bottom of baking pan. Reserve another ½ cup kasseri cheese for sprinkling over the top of the Béchamel Sauce.

5. In a large bowl, combine the macaroni, vegetables, and all remaining ingredients with salt and pepper. Mix well. Transfer mixture to the prepared baking pan.

6. Bake in preheated 350°F oven for 15 minutes. Remove pan; set aside to cool. Lower oven temperature to 325°F.

7. Meanwhile, prepare Béchamel Sauce (see recipe below). Using a rubber spatula, spread the Béchamel Sauce on top of the Vegetarian Pastitsio so all areas are covered. Sprinkle top with the reserved ½ cup grated kasseri cheese.

8. Bake in preheated 325°F oven for 30 to 35 minutes, until the top turns golden brown.

SALADS

ATHENIAN SALAD

Shredded romaine lettuce, fresh green onions, dill, crumbled Greek feta, and a delicious vinaigrette with oregano and garlic combine to make this Athenian Salad a most refreshing menu item (see Parthenon Favorites, p. 117). It is delightful, cleanses the palate, and is compatible with many hearty meals.

YIELD: 4 SERVINGS

1 medium head (about 1 pound) romaine lettuce, rinsed, dried, shredded

4 to 5 green onions, sliced

4 ounces quality Greek feta cheese, crumbled

About ⅔ cup (5 large sprigs) finely chopped fresh dill

8 tomato wedges

½ recipe Greek Salad Dressing (recipe follows)

1. In a large salad bowl, add all ingredients except Greek Salad Dressing and toss carefully.

2. Pour ½ recipe of Greek Salad Dressing over salad, tossing carefully to moisten.

3. Store any remaining dressing for the next Greek Salad, Village Salad, or Athenian Salad (see recipes, pp. 80, 81, and 77).

GREEK SALAD DRESSING

YIELD: ABOUT ¾ CUP DRESSING

½ cup extra virgin olive oil

1½ tablespoons red wine vinegar

1½ tablespoons white wine vinegar

1 clove garlic, finely chopped

1 tablespoon crumbled, dried oregano

1 teaspoon salt

1 teaspoon freshly ground black pepper

In a small bowl, add all ingredients and whisk well. Set aside 20 minutes for flavors to blend. Store leftovers covered at room temperature.

ATHENIAN SALAD

GREEK SALAD

This refreshing Greek Salad is a wonderful addition to a vegetarian meal (see p. 113) or to most any other Mediterranean menus. The iceberg lettuce makes it more American in origin, but it segues into many contemporary Greek meals. Cucumber slices, tomato wedges, green bell pepper strips, peperoncini, Kalamata olives, and feta cheese all contribute to an attractive, substantial salad with texture and flavor. The Greek Salad Dressing bathes it in a delicious herbal-tart olive oil blend.

YIELD: 4 SERVINGS

½ recipe Greek Salad Dressing (see p. 77)

1 head iceberg lettuce, cored, rinsed, torn into bite-sized pieces

½ cucumber, peeled, cut in half lengthwise, then sliced ½-inch thick

2 medium tomatoes, halved, seeded, cut into ½-inch-thick wedges.

1 large green bell pepper, stemmed, halved, seeded, cut into ½-inch wide strips

4 peperoncini

15 Kalamata olives

Salt to taste, optional

4 to 5 ounces quality Greek feta cheese, cut into squares or crumbled

Garnish: Several thin strips red bell pepper (optional)

1. Prepare Greek Salad Dressing and set aside for flavors to blend.

2. In a large salad bowl or platter, combine all salad ingredients except cheese and pepper strips, tossing carefully. Arrange feta over top. Garnish with red pepper strips.

3. Pour half of the Greek Salad Dressing over salad, tossing carefully to moisten.

4. Store any remaining dressing for the next Greek Salad, Village Salad, or Athenian Salad (see recipes, pp. 80, 81, and 77).

VILLAGE SALAD

Colorful, chunky, and flavored with Kalamata olives, Greek feta, and a vinaigrette dressing sparked with garlic and oregano, the Village Salad is satisfying with crusty bread, a bowl of soup, or an appetizer for lunch. It also makes a great starter for many dinners. Since it is made without lettuce, leftovers keep well for another day when covered and chilled.

YIELD: 4 SERVINGS

½ recipe Greek Salad Dressing (see p. 77)

1 cucumber, peeled, cut in half lengthwise, then sliced ½-inch thick

1 small sweet onion, peeled, halved, cut into thin slivers

3 medium tomatoes, halved, seeded, cut into ½-inch thick wedges.

1 large green bell pepper, stemmed, halved, seeded, cut into ½-inch wide strips

15 Kalamata olives

4 to 5 ounces quality Greek feta cheese, crumbled

Salt to taste (optional)

1. Prepare Greek Salad Dressing and set aside for flavors to blend.

2. In a large salad bowl, combine all ingredients for salad, tossing carefully.

3. Pour half the Greek Salad Dressing over salad ingredients, tossing carefully to moisten.

4. Store any remaining dressing for the next Greek Salad, Village Salad, or Athenian Salad (see recipes, pp. 80, 81, and 77).

VILLAGE SALAD

THE SIDE DISHES

THE PARTHENON'S FAMOUS BRAISED EGGPLANT

Braised vegetables are popular in Greek cuisine, and The Parthenon offers several, including this famous Braised Eggplant recipe, Braised Green Beans, and Braised Okra (see photo, p. 88). Eggplant requires a bit more preparation with soaking and sautéing first, but it is well worth the effort. Taste the delicious results and you'll understand why it has so many enthusiastic fans.

YIELD: 4 TO 6 SIDE-DISH SERVINGS*

4 medium eggplants

Salted water

¾ cup olive oil (as needed), divided

1 medium yellow onion, chopped

1 cup chopped tomatoes (2 medium)

2 teaspoons chopped (2 cloves) garlic

¼ cup tomato paste

2 cups water

1 tablespoon chopped fresh flat-leaf parsley

Salt and freshly ground black pepper to taste

1. Halve eggplants lengthwise; cut each half into 4 equal pieces (32 pieces total). In a large bowl ½ to ⅔ full of salted water, submerge eggplant in salted water for ½ to 1 hour. Remove eggplant, rinse thoroughly, and pat dry with paper towels.

2. Reserve 2 tablespoons olive oil for step 4. In a large skillet, add 1 tablespoon of the olive oil, heat over medium heat; sauté 4 eggplant slices (or whatever fits in the bottom of the skillet) until they lightly brown on 1 side; turn to brown on other side, adding a little more oil if necessary. Remove and drain on paper towels. Transfer to platter and keep warm. Repeat procedure with 1 tablespoon oil and another batch of eggplant until all eggplant is browned.

3. Preheat oven to 375°F.

4. To a large, ovenproof 9 x 13-inch baking pan, add the remaining 2 tablespoons olive oil and heat over medium heat on a top burner. Sauté onion, tomatoes, and garlic, stirring with wooden spoon, until transparent, about 5 minutes. Arrange the prepared eggplant over the top of the onion-tomato mixture.

5. In a small bowl or 2-cup glass measure, stir the tomato paste in 2 cups of water until blended; add the parsley, salt, and pepper to the diluted tomato paste and pour evenly over ingredients in pan. Mix gently, place pan in preheated 375°F oven and bake for about 1 hour, until eggplant is tender and golden brown.

*NOTE: The Parthenon's servings are very generous. This recipe will easily serve 8 to 10 as a side dish.

BRAISED OKRA

Okra is sometimes called "gumbo," because it serves as a thickener in a Louisiana gumbo. This unique vegetable has a viscous liquid that is released upon moist, slow cooking. For the Braised Okra, Chef Sotiris first boils the okra in a red wine vinegar-water mixture to remove most of the thick juice and then sautés it briefly with onion and garlic. Next, it simmers in a tomato sauce until it is soft and the flavors have blended. Braised Okra is a great side with Tigania *(see Parthenon Favorites, p. 117) and is an appropriate green vegetable on the Combination Plate in the Vegetarian Meal (see p. 113).*

YIELD: 4 SIDE-DISH SERVINGS*

To prepare for cooking:

    1 pound okra, rinsed

    ½ cup red wine vinegar

    1½ cups water

To cook:

    ⅓ cup olive oil

    ½ medium (about ½ cup) onion, chopped

    1 garlic clove, chopped

    1 tablespoon tomato paste

    1 cup water

    ½ teaspoon salt

    ¼ teaspoon freshly ground black pepper

    1 teaspoon sugar

1. Place okra in a medium saucepan with the ½ cup red wine vinegar and 1½ cups of water. Bring to boil over high heat; reduce heat to medium, cover and boil about 10 minutes. Remove from heat; drain okra, rinsing well with cool tap water. Set aside.

2. In a large skillet, heat the olive oil over medium heat. When hot, sauté onion and garlic until transparent. Add okra, stirring well to combine; sauté briefly.

3. In a small bowl or 1-cup glass measure, dissolve the tomato paste in the 1 cup water, stirring well. Add salt, pepper, and sugar, stirring to blend. Add mixture to the pot with the okra, stirring well to combine.

4. Bring to a boil over medium-high heat; reduce heat, cover, and simmer for about 40 minutes, or until the okra is tender and cooked to your liking.

*NOTE: This recipe may be doubled.

THE PARTHENON'S FAMOUS BRAISED GREEN BEANS

Greek–style Braised Green Beans are slow-cooked; the ingredients are simmered until the green beans soften and absorb the flavors of onion, tomatoes, garlic, and other herbs. It makes a wonderful side dish to Braised Lamb (see Parthenon Favorites, p. 117) and would be a terrific addition to any Greek party (see Greek Party Menu, p. 116).

YIELD: 4 SIDE-DISH SERVINGS*

⅓ cup olive oil

1 medium (about 1 cup) onion, chopped

3 garlic cloves, chopped

2 medium tomatoes, peeled and finely chopped

2 bay leaves

2 pounds green beans, rinsed, stems removed

2 teaspoons sugar

½ cup chopped parsley

3 tablespoons tomato paste

2 cups water

1. Place olive oil in a large pan over medium-low heat. Add the chopped onion and garlic; sauté until the onions turn translucent, about 2 minutes. Add all of the ingredients except the tomato paste and water.

2. Cover and cook over low heat until the beans become slightly soft, about 10 minutes.

3. In a small bowl or 2-cup glass measure, dissolve the tomato paste in the 2 cups water, stirring well. Add this mixture to the beans in the pot.

4. Stir; bring to a simmer over medium heat, then cover, reduce heat, and cook over low heat for about 1 hour or until the beans are soft and cooked to your liking. Remove bay leaves and serve hot.

*NOTE: The Parthenon's servings are very generous. This recipe will easily serve 6 to 8 as a side dish.

GREEK ROASTED POTATOES

Customers love these potatoes so much that many request the recipe. They are simple to prepare at home and enhance most roasted main dishes (see Greek Party Menu, p. 116). The Parthenon serves Greek Roasted Potatoes with items that are roasted, broiled, and rotisseried, including Roast Leg or Loin of Lamb, Rotisserie-Roasted Lamb, Athenian Broiled Chicken, Rotisserie-Roasted Chicken, Chicken Souvlaki, and Pork Souvlaki.

4 large baking potatoes, cut lengthwise in quarters

3 to 4 tablespoons fresh lemon juice

⅓ cup extra virgin olive oil

2 teaspoons salt

1½ teaspoons freshly ground black pepper

1 tablespoon dried oregano

1 plum tomato, chopped

1. Preheat oven to 450°F.

2. Arrange potatoes in large baking dish with all ingredients except tomatoes. Mix well. Add water to baking dish until halfway up the potatoes. Arrange tomatoes evenly over the top. Cover top with foil.

3. Bake in preheated oven about 1½ hours, or until potatoes are soft. Remove foil and bake a few more minutes until potatoes are slightly browned on top. Serve hot.

RICE PILAFI

In addition to Greek Roasted Potatoes, another popular side dish at The Parthenon is Rice Pilafi. It is served with most seafood main dishes, braised dishes, and alongside potatoes with many other items. There are many requests for the recipe, but it is surprisingly simple. Here are the directions from Chef Sotiris.

Converted rice

Salted boiling water

Bay leaf

Butter

1. Use converted rice,* following the package's directions and estimating the servings needed.

2. Add a bay leaf to the pot and a teaspoon of butter per serving, which melts in the salted boiling water and coats the rice.

3. Remove the bay leaf before serving.

* The Parthenon uses Uncle Ben's Converted Rice. Converted rice is whole-grain rice that has been parboiled before milling. It retains many nutrients that otherwise would be lost in the milling process and requires slightly longer cooking times than regular rice.

CLOCKWISE FROM TOP LEFT:
BRAISED OKRA · BRAISED GREEN BEANS · BRAISED EGGPLANT

Soups

Avgolemono Soupa (Egg-Lemon Soup)

The tart lemony taste of this chicken stock–based soup thickened with eggs simultaneously whets the appetite and satisfies. It's difficult to pass up a second helping (see Traditional Greek Meal, p. 112).

YIELD: 4 BOWL OR 6 CUP SERVINGS

6 cups water
½ cup chicken base
1 cup uncooked long-grain rice, washed
3 eggs, separated, at room temperature
¼ cup fresh lemon juice
2 tablespoons cornstarch
Lemon wedges

1. Bring the water and chicken base to a boil; stir to blend. Add rice. Bring to a boil again, reduce heat, cover, and simmer for 15 minutes. Remove from heat.

2. Measure out 3 cups of the stock from the rice mixture into a small saucepan. Keep warm over low heat.

3. In a large mixing bowl, beat the egg whites with an electric beater until white and frothy, like a soft meringue. Add the yolks, lemon juice, and cornstarch; continue beating until cornstarch dissolves.

4. Gradually add the 3 cups of stock while continuing to beat the egg mixture. Beat for a few more minutes. Stir egg mixture into hot rice soup, blending thoroughly. If a thicker consistency is desired, add 1½ teaspoons cornstarch; stir and heat 1 minute. Serve hot with lemon wedges.

BEEF AND ORZO SOUP

This hearty beef soup brims with vegetables and is enhanced by orzo, a pasta that resembles rice in shape and size. The soup is available at The Parthenon on Tuesdays and Thursdays in both cup and bowl portions. It is simple to prepare, and the leftovers are wonderful for several days. It's especially therapeutic on a brisk day (see Parthenon Favorites, p. 117).

YIELD: ABOUT 4½ QUARTS; 8 TO 10 BOWL SERVINGS; 16 TO 18 CUP SERVINGS

1½ pounds beef shoulder

2 quarts plus 1 cup water

2 cups cubed raw potatoes

2 cups chopped celery

1 cup chopped carrot

2 cups chopped onion

1 cup tomato paste

1½ teaspoons salt

½ teaspoon freshly ground black pepper

1 cup orzo

1. To a large pot, add beef, 2 quarts water, and all the vegetables. Bring to boil, reduce heat to low, and simmer for 1½ hours.

2. Add tomato paste, salt, and pepper and continue cooking for ½ hour.

3. Remove only the beef from the pot. Add orzo, cover, and continue cooking for 20 minutes. If the soup gets too thick, add another cup of water.

4. Chop beef into small cubes while the orzo cooks.

5. When the orzo finishes cooking (after 20 minutes), return the cubed beef to the orzo mixture and simmer for 5 minutes.

6. Ladle soup into bowls. Serve hot.

NAVY BEAN SOUP

Although it is one of the most popular openers at The Parthenon, Navy Bean Soup is prepared only three days a week: Wednesdays, Fridays, and Sundays. Like all other soups, it is available in both cup or bowl sizes. The beans are infused with onion, celery, and carrot flavors, as well as the tomato base. A bowlful of this hearty soup is warming and filling. With little more than crusty bread and an appetizer or salad, it's the basis of a simple, satisfying meal.

YIELD: ABOUT 3 QUARTS SOUP; 6 BOWL SERVINGS; 12 CUP SERVINGS

1 onion, chopped

1 cup chopped, peeled celery

1 cup chopped carrots

Boiling water

2 cups dried navy beans

¾ cup extra virgin olive oil

2½ teaspoons salt, or to taste

2 teaspoons freshly ground black pepper, or to taste

2 tablespoons tomato paste diluted in 1 cup water

1 handful (about ⅓ cup) chopped parsley

1. In a large saucepan, add chopped onion, celery, and carrots to boiling water—just enough to cover vegetables. Cover and cook over low heat for 45 minutes. Using a slotted spoon, remove vegetables and transfer to a strainer; drain and reserve. Reserve vegetable broth in pot.

2. In a medium saucepan, add beans to 2 cups water and bring to a boil. Cover and continue boiling over medium heat for 1 hour. The beans will be about half cooked and will expand in volume. Using a slotted spoon, remove beans from water and transfer to a colander. Rinse well. Reserve.

3. Measure 1 quart vegetable broth in the first large saucepan. Add reserved vegetables, beans, oil, salt, and pepper; stir. Bring to boil, cover, and continue boiling for ½ hour. Add diluted tomato paste mixture; stir well. Continue boiling for another ½ hour or until beans are soft. Remove from heat, cover, and allow soup flavors to blend for 10 minutes. Adjust seasoning.

4. Ladle soup into bowls; sprinkle each serving with chopped parsley.

DESSERTS

BAKLAVA (HONEY-NUT PASTRY)

Baklava is the quintessential Greek (and Middle Eastern) pastry. It's a rich layered mixture of cinnamon-and-sugar-coated walnuts and buttered phyllo baked until the pastry is crisp and then soaked in a hot, spiced honey syrup. After you taste it (once it's cooled, of course), you'll see why it deserves its position as the embodiment of Greek pastry. Strong Greek coffee is a perfect accompaniment (see Greek Party Menu, p. 116, and Parthenon Favorites, p. 117).

YIELD: 15 TO 18 SERVINGS

For filling:

>   4 cups chopped walnuts
>   ½ cup sugar
>   1 teaspoon ground cinnamon

For pastry:

>   1 pound phyllo pastry leaves*
>   ½ cup melted unsalted butter (1 stick)

For syrup:

>   1 cup sugar
>   ¾ cup honey
>   1½ cups water
>   1 cinnamon stick
>   2 cloves

1. Preheat oven to 325°F.

2. To a medium bowl, add chopped walnuts, the ½ cup sugar, and the 1 teaspoon of cinnamon. Mix together.

3. Generously butter a 9 x 13-inch pan. Begin layering the phyllo leaves (folded in half if necessary), turning edges under to fit the pan, and brushing melted butter over each phyllo leaf. Do the same for 8 layers of phyllo leaves (4 leaves if you are folding them), but do not butter the top leaf. Sprinkle evenly with 2 cups of the walnut mixture.

4. Continue the same procedure with 3 more layers of phyllo leaves and walnut mixture until 2 or 3 leaves are left. Place these remaining leaves on top of each other, buttering each one. Smooth over outer surface with remaining butter, and sprinkle with a little water. Using a sharp serrated knife, cut the baklava lengthwise into desired even, rectangular rows, then vent each row about every half inch.

GREEK YOGURT WITH HONEY AND WALNUTS

RIZOGALO (RICE PUDDING)

When I first tasted The Parthenon's rice pudding, it brought back childhood memories. This is a custardy, smooth rice creation with a cinnamon scent. It's comfort food to me, but this is a dessert for all ages. The Parthenon serves it elegantly in a tall pedestal dessert dish (see Parthenon Favorites and photo, pp. 117 and 107). However you serve it, we're sure you and your guests will love it.

YIELD: 8 TO 10 OR MORE SERVINGS

1 cup converted rice*

1 quart water

6 cups milk

1 cup sugar

1 navel orange, unpeeled, rinsed, quartered, seeded

Ground cinnamon

1. Wash and rinse rice very well in strainer; drain.

2. In large (3- to 4-quart) saucepan, bring 1 quart water to a boil. Add the rice, bring to a boil, reduce heat, and cook over medium-high heat until almost all of the water is gone. Add the milk, sugar, and orange quarters; stir well. Cover and simmer over low heat until mixture thickens, about 1¼ hours.

3. Remove the orange and discard. Pour pudding into 6-ounce pedestal dessert dishes or serving dishes. Allow to cool. Cover with plastic wrap and refrigerate 2 or more hours.

4. When ready to serve, remove plastic wrap and lightly dust pudding with ground cinnamon.

*Uncle Ben's converted rice is used at The Parthenon. If using another rice, follow package directions.

GREEK YOGURT WITH HONEY AND WALNUTS

Greek yogurt drizzled with flavorful golden honey and sprinkled with walnuts is most refreshing after a big meal, and it is one of the healthiest desserts in any cuisine. This creation is an example of the joy of simple food.

YIELD: 4 DESSERTS

2 cups thick, quality Greek yogurt

¼ cup quality honey

24 walnut halves

Divide yogurt into four dessert bowls. Drizzle honey evenly over the yogurt. Sprinkle each serving with 6 walnuts.

A Traditional Greek meal, clockwise from top left: Yogurt with honey and walnuts · Avgolemono Soupa · Tzatziki · Pastitsio · Roast Leg of Lamb Garnished with Rice Pilafi and Roasted Potatoes · Taramosalata · Village Salad

A Vegetarian Meal, clockwise from top left: Rizogalo · Pan-Fried Zucchini with Skordalia · Tirosalata · Cold Bean Plate · Vegetarian Combination Plate (Vegetarian Moussaka, Braised Okra, Vegetarian Pastitsio, and Rice Pilafi) · Village Salad

Food and Wine Pairing Tips

Many factors affect the selection of foods and wines. For example, the environment in which you experience a wine is very important. During warm weather, most people prefer chilled white wines with light fare; in winter, full red wines and heartier dishes are frequent favorites. A wine you enjoyed with a good friend in a beautiful setting might taste different later, in a less amenable business setting. Balance in lifestyle also plays a role. For example, after returning from a trip that included many sumptuous meals, most people simplify their diets and eat lighter fare.

Your first reaction to a wine's aroma and taste is important, and that's usually what prevails. Pay attention to that first impression: Taste the wine alone, and then taste it with food, noting any change in perception. Discovering your preference is a subjective process.

Opposites: Contrasts, such as sour-salty, sweet-salty, and sweet-sour, can be delightful, as well. For example, a wine with a good acidic (tart) quality, such as a crisp, dry white Greek wine, pairs well with the salty, fatty fish roe in Taramosalata (see p. 32).

Balance: The sweetness or sourness of a dish should be lower than the sweetness or acidity of the wine; otherwise, it will change the perception of the full fruit-acid balance of the wine. For example, a salad with just a touch of vinegar or lemon juice in its dressing would be compatible with a dry white Greek wine.

The bitter tastes of high-tannin red wines are more compatible with fattier foods. The fat coats the tongue and softens the bitterness, so the fat and the bitter make a happy marriage (for food and wine—not necessarily for people). It is usually safe to pair a full-bodied, oak-aged red wine with a hearty meat course.

Spicy foods are best with low-alcohol, fruity, or off-dry whites and low-tannin reds.

Serving Wine

In general, people usually serve white wines too cold and red wines too warm, and they sometimes ignore the recommended order for serving wines—from light to full to sweet. Although adventurous souls can always bend the rules, for overall optimum flavor enjoyment, use the following guidelines for serving wines at your party.

Optimum serving temperatures for wines:

- Sparkling wine—cold, refrigerator temperature (40–45°F).

- White wine—a bit warmer than refrigerator temperature (about 55°F)

- Red wine—cool room temperature (about 65°F)

Suggested order of serving wines: It would be unlikely that all of the following wines would be served at any one event, but the suggested order of serving is helpful to get maximum taste enjoyment. The beauty of a Brut sparkling wine or Champagne is its versatility, as it can be served throughout the meal; a demi-sec sparkling wine pairs with desserts. Off-dry whites and reds tend to be fruity but not very sweet; however, depending on the individual wines, you might position them differently after your initial tasting.

Brut sparkling wines
Dry whites
Off-dry whites
Dry light reds
Dry medium-bodied reds
Dry full-bodied reds
Demi-sec sparkling wines
Off-dry reds
Sweet wines

A Greek Seaside Taverna Menu,
clockwise from top left: Pan-Fried Kalamari
Cold Octopus Salad · Fried Codfish with Skordalia
Taramosalata · Broiled Red Snapper · Stuffed Squid

THE MENUS

YANNA LIAKOURAS CAREFULLY PLANNED THESE MENUS, BASED ON GREEK tradition, typical meals (e.g., Seaside Taverna), and Parthenon favorites. Many of the items in each menu can be prepared in advance, leaving several to be finalized just before serving. And remember: Entertaining is always easier when family and friends bring an item or two. You can always select just a few favorites on any of Yanna's menus, streamlining the preparation according to your available time and kitchen equipment. Wine suggestions are also offered to simplify your planning, but the final decision is yours, based on availability, your preference, and that of your guests. *Kali orexi* (good appetite)!

A Traditional Greek Meal

Yanna recommends this traditional Greek menu for a home gathering, such as a birthday or anniversary celebration. Some holiday meals might incorporate several of these dishes, as well. The menu offers varied choices and is relatively simple to produce, since several items can be prepared in advance.

Taramosalata (fish roe spread), see p. 32

Tzatziki (yogurt-cucumber-garlic dip), see p. 34

Avgolemono Soupa (egg-lemon soup), see p. 90

Village Salad, see p. 81

Pastitsio, see p. 64

Roast Leg of Lamb, see p. 57

Rice Pilafi, see p. 87

Yogurt with Honey and Walnuts, see p. 98

Wine suggestions: with the first courses, it's best to choose a dry white Greek wine, like Boutari Lac des Roches, a golden, 100% Savatiano varietal with a fresh, fruity character and soft structure. The wine is well-balanced with acidiy that refreshes the palate after salty fish roe and garlic.

With the Pastitsio and Roast Leg of Lamb, I recommend a 2005 Saint George (varietal: Aghiorgitiko), which is a dry, medium-bodied red. It has a deep red color, hints of sweet oak on the nose (from one year in barrels), and hardy tannins. The wine is frank and intense.

A Vegetarian Meal

Whether or not you and your guests are vegetarians, everyone enjoys these winners. The cold items—Cold Bean Salad, Tirosalata, and Greek Salad—are all quite different, providing a nice array of flavors and textures. The hot, crispy Pan-Fried Zucchini with Skordalia (cold, smooth, puréed garlic potatoes) is a study in contrasts. The main-course combination plate of Vegetarian Moussaka and Pastitsio and the Braised Okra add flavor and substance. Creamy Rizogalo is an appropriate ending.

Cold Bean Salad, see p. 27

Tirosalata (cheese spread), see p. 33

Greek Salad, see p. 80

Pan-Fried Zucchini with Skordalia (Greek puréed potatoes with garlic), see p. 38

Combination Plate: Vegetarian Moussaka, Vegetarian Pastitsio, and Braised Okra,
    see pp. 73, 76, and 85

Rizogalo (rice pudding), see p. 98

Wine suggestion: Agioritiko White, Tsantali. This dry white wine, a blend of the homegrown varietals Assyrtiko, Athiri, and Roditis, has a clear yellow-gold color, flavors of peaches and green apples, and a lively kick on the palate.)

A Greek Seaside Taverna Menu

Yanna says, "This menu typifies what might be eaten on the outdoor patio at a seaside taverna in Greece. For dessert, there'd be little more than some fresh fruit." When preparing this at home, you can shorten the menu by selecting one or two of the four main courses.

Taramosalata (fish roe spread), see p. 32

Cold Octopus Salad, see p. 28

Stuffed Squid, see p. 69

Pan-fried Kalamari, see p. 39

Broiled Red Snapper, see p. 45

Fried Codfish with Skordalia (Greek puréed potatoes with garlic), see p. 62

Wine suggestions: Moshofilero, Boutari, 2006. This is a premium dry white wine from 100 percent Moshofilero grapes. Its brilliant, clear white-yellow color has a greenish tint. Its fresh, intense floral and fruity bouquet is dominated by aromas of rose, melon, and citrus. It also has a long aftertaste of orange blossoms and grapefruit.

Stuffed Squid can be paired with a red wine, like Boutari Lac des Roches, a medium-bodied, fruit-forward wine with modest tannins.

PARTHENON FAVORITES, CLOCKWISE FROM LEFT:
ATHENIAN SALAD · SAGANAKI · GREEK MEAT SAUCE WITH SPAGHETTI
TIGANIA WITH BRAISEDOKRA · BRAISED LAMB WITH BRAISED GREEN BEANS
CHICKEN SOUVLAKI · WITH RICE PILAFI · BEEF AND ORZO SOUP

GREEK FOOD GLOSSARY

Avgolemono Saltsa—a tart egg-lemon sauce made of eggs, lemon juice, and chicken stock that is served with the dishes Lamb with Artichokes and Dolmades.

Avgolemono Soupa—a tart egg-lemon soup with rice and chicken stock.

Baklava—flaky phyllo pastry layered with nuts and spices—especially cinnamon—and steeped in syrup.

Dolmades—stuffed grape vine leaves. They can be made as smaller, rice-filled appetizers or larger meat-and-rice-filled rolls. Served with Avgolemono Saltsa.

Feta—a salty, crumbly, brined white cheese made from sheep's, goat's, or cow's milk. It is used in salads, sauces, and fillings for foods like Spanakotyropita or Tyropita.

Galaktoboureko—custard and flaky phyllo pastry soaked in orange-flavored syrup.

Giouvetsi—Roast Leg of Lamb with Orzo (a tiny oval pasta that resembles rice).

Gyros—a blend of seasoned beef and lamb roasted on a giant, slowly rotating spit.

Kasseri—a firm, light-yellow cheese made from sheep's milk.

Kefalotiri—a hard, light yellow, grating cheese, similar to Parmesan, that is made from sheep's or goat's milk.

Kota Kapama—chicken braised in a sweet spice-flavored (nutmeg or cinnamon) Tomato Sauce.

Melitzanosalata—a thick eggplant salad/spread made with baked eggplant, parsley, garlic, olive oil, and red wine vinegar; served as a cold appetizer with bread.

Metaxa—a Greek brandy that is available in several ages and styles.

Mezedes—small plates or first-course dishes. The Parthenon offers most of them in two sizes. Traditionally, Greeks enjoy getting together with friends to talk, eat several mezedes, and drink wine. A diner may order a meze as an appetizer or a light meal.

Mezes—small portion of something (e.g., a small portion from a main course).

Moussaka—traditional layered casserole/pie of eggplant slices and meat sauce topped and baked with Béchamel Sauce. It is also served with Tomato Sauce. The vegetarian version substitutes vegetables for the meat and is topped with Béchamel Sauce, but it is not served with Tomato Sauce. There are many variations.

Olive oil—the key cooking fat of the country, produced in several styles. Extra virgin olive oil is best for salads and drizzling over dishes, but regular olive oil is more suitable for cooking.

Olives—there are many varieties and shades of Greek olives, including the popular black Kalamata. Olives are used in many different salads and mezedes and garnish entrees as well.

Ouzo—a strong anise-flavored aperitif.

Pastitsio—a traditional casserole dish made with macaroni #2 (special long noodles found in Greek groceries) and meat sauce. It is topped with Béchamel Sauce and baked, then served with tomato sauce. The vegetarian version substitutes vegetables for the meat and also includes Béchamel Sauce, but it is not served with Tomato Sauce.

Saganaki—traditionally, melted cheese; Chris Liakouras embellished it by pouring Metaxa over a serving of kasseri cheese, setting it alight, and shouting, "Oopa!" Today, Chris's contemporary flambéed version is nationally known. The Parthenon prefers using kasseri cheese to the saltier kefalotiri cheese used at many other restaurants.

Skordalia—a garlic sauce made of mashed potatoes, olive oil, and lemon juice; traditionally served with codfish.

Souvlaki—refers to all types of broiled or grilled shish kebob, including meat, chicken, or fish. Souvlaki is one shish kebob; souvlakia is plural.

Spanakotyropita—spinach-cheese phyllo pies, served hot as small triangular pies as an appetizer, or cut into pieces when baked in a large pan and served as a meze.

Taramosalata—a fish-roe spread that is combined with moistened bread and whipped until smooth with lemon juice and olive oil.

Tyropita—a cheese phyllo pie, sometimes called a "cheese puff," that is served hot as an appetizer or meze (appetizer).

Tirosalata—a cheese salad made with feta and ricotta cheeses, chopped bell peppers, and several herbs, including dill, parsley, and garlic; it is served as a cold appetizer.

Tzatziki—a cold dip made of garlic-flavored yogurt mixed with chopped cucumber. Served as a meze (appetizer) or as an accompaniment to gyros.

Acknowledgments and Credits

A big thank you to all who have contributed their information, expertise, talents, and assistance to this book: the photographers, recipe testers, The Parthenon team (Yanna Liakouras devoted a lot of time to work closely with me on this book) and all those I have interviewed, including The Parthenon's waiters.

Thank you to Harry Mark Petrakis for his personal remembrance of Chris Liakouras and The Parthenon.

In addition to myself, the following contributors tested the recipes in this book. A big thank you to: Sandra Falco, who loves cooking and is passionate about food and wine, and who, while working toward a culinary degree, has become one of my most enthusiastic College of DuPage students; Barbara Modzalewska, who loves trying new recipes at home and works in the catering business; and Maya Norris, the managing editor of a restaurant industry trade magazine and a wonderful cook.

Thanks to writer/editor Martha Conger, who constructed the Index.

Special thanks to Doug Seibold of Agate Publishing for his strong interest in this project when it was just a proposal, for his vision of the finished book, and for his suggestions and support during the process. We were working under a tight deadline, and he granted a needed extension. And special recognition goes to his talented staff, especially Perrin Davis, who made this cookbook a reality.

Thank you to the staff at the Hellenic Museum & Cultural Center. They were immensely helpful to me when I was doing research for the history portion of this book, and they have been most enthusiastic and supportive of this project. Special thanks go to Sophia Kintis, executive director; Allison Heller-Fluecke, collections manager; Antonia Lekas, librarian; and Peter Georgalan, communications manager.

Thanks to Alexa Ganakos, publisher and executive editor of GreekCircle magazine and author of *Greektown Chicago: Its History—Its Recipes*, for her assistance with contacts.

Thanks to those involved with Special Service Area (SSA) #16, Greektown (in lieu of a Greektown Chamber of Commerce), including Dean Maragos, who was involved in the beautification program of Greektown and supplied valuable information, and Frank J. Caputo, Commissioner for SSA #16 Greektown, who sent information on the current Greektown.

Thanks to Lowell B. Komie, attorney and author, for his counsel.

Thanks to all my family and friends for their understanding and support during this project.

From Chris Liakouras, the Liakouras family, and Chef Sotiris:

In the spring of 2007, our friend Camille Stagg suggested that we do a cookbook to commemorate The Parthenon's 40th anniversary. We loved the idea. Once we decided to move forward with it, we selected her to coordinate and write our book, since she has had a long association with The Parthenon and understands the cuisine, our menu, and our history. We have a feeling of love and friendship for her and never even considered anyone else to tell our story.

PHOTOGRAPHY CREDITS

Food and restaurant interior photos by Rich Foreman of Rich Foreman Photography—Rich Foreman, principal, and Elliot Burlingham, photo assistant.

Author photo by Rich Malec, College of DuPage.

Other photos courtesy of Hellenic Museum & Cultural Center and The Parthenon Restaurant, as credited.

BIBLIOGRAPHY

Ganakos, Alexa. *Greektown Chicago: Its History—Its Recipes*, G. Bradley Publishing, 2005.

Greek National Tourist Organization. *Greece 1990.*

Karras, Angela R. "Chicago's Greek Town Renovation Plans Nearing Completion," first in a series, November 30, 1995, *The Greek Star.*

Nickles, Harry G., and the Editors of Time-Life Books. "Greece: The Meeting of East and West," *Middle Eastern Cooking*, Time Inc., 1969.

"Opaa! The Parthenon Turns 35," July 31, 2003, *The Greek Star.*

Poulos, Terry. "Parthenon Still Blazing Trails 30 Years Later," July 23, 1998, *The Greek Star.*

Stagg, Camille. *Cooking with Wine: Flavorful Recipes and Tips on Serving Wines with Food*, Time-Life Books, 1997.

Stagg, Camille. *The Eclectic Gourmet Guide to Chicago, 2nd Edition*, Menasha Ridge Press, 2000.

About the Author

Camille Stagg is a food and travel journalist, editor, teacher, and consultant with more than 35 years of experience. She is the former food editor for *Cuisine* magazine and for the *Chicago Sun-Times*, where she won awards for excellence in food journalism. She has been a dining critic and contributor for numerous other publications and has appeared frequently on television and radio. She has traveled extensively on assignments (visiting Greece three times). An award-winning teacher of culinary classes with wine pairings at College of DuPage, Glen Ellyn, Illinois, she has also won numerous professional recipe awards. This is the sixteenth book she has contributed to or authored.

INDEX